PRAISE FOR
The Queen of Clean

"Linda Cobb, the self-styled Queen of Clean®, sweeps into the big time with spotless timing for a book on dirt. . . . *Talking Dirty with the Queen of Clean®* . . . has certainly cleaned up."

—*People*

"There's no stain Linda Cobb can't tame."

—*New York Post*

"Let's face it, cleanup problems are a stain on all of us, but since the Queen has been on the show we have all become sponges, soaking up every drop of information she has."

—Dan Davis, *Good Morning Arizona*,
KTVK-TV, Phoenix

"There isn't any stain or cleaning problem for which Cobb doesn't have a solution. . . ."

—*The Arizona Republic*

"We all look for solutions to life's little accidents that spot our daily lives. Linda helps with simple remedies using everyday products. *Talking Dirty with the Queen of Clean®* is a must-read and a book to have at your side at all times. You're in for a real treat."

—John Nuzzo, WBVP Radio,
Beaver Falls, Pennsylvania

Please Note: I hope this advice provides the answers to many of your household needs. However, total success cannot be guaranteed in every case. Care and caution should be exercised when using remedies, products, and methods presented in this book. All cleaning treatments should be tested prior to application, in an inconspicuous place. This is highly recommended and strongly encouraged. Please read and follow all information contained on product labels with care. Linda Cobb, The Win Holden Company, and Pocket Books hereby disclaim any liability and damages from the use and/or misuse of any product, formula, or application presented in this book.

You too can be a Queen for All Seasons!

Also by Linda Cobb

Talking Dirty Laundry with the Queen of Clean®
Talking Dirty with the Queen of Clean®

A Queen for All Seasons

A Year of Tips, Tricks, and Picks
for a Cleaner House
and a More Organized Life!

LINDA COBB

POCKET BOOKS

New York London Toronto Sydney Singapore

An *Original* Publication of POCKET BOOKS

 POCKET BOOKS, a division of Simon & Schuster, Inc.
1230 Avenue of the Americas, New York, NY 10020

ISBN: 0-7434-2831-5

First Pocket Books trade paperback printing October 2001

10   9   8   7   6   5   4   3   2   1

Queen of Clean® is the registered trademark of Linda Cobb and is the property of Queen and King Enterprises, Inc.

POCKET and colophon are registered trademarks of Simon & Schuster, Inc.

For information regarding special discounts for bulk purchases, please contact Simon & Schuster Special Sales at 1-800-456-6798 or business@simonandschuster.com

Book design by Helene Berinsky

Cover design by Lisa Litwack
Photo credits: author photos by John Hall, other photos by C Squared Studios/GettyOne

Printed in the U.S.A.

Thanks

John. You are soft-spoken; I am a chatterbox. You love to sing; I love to laugh. You sang will you marry me, and I shouted yes! You have made my heart smile every day since.

The Queen Mother. You continue to amaze and inspire me. The pride and love in your eyes when you look at me is all I will ever need.

Dad, I look over my shoulder and know you are still there.

Our kids and their families who put up with our crazy life. We love you—and even more, we like you.

Duane Dooling, who gifted me with the title for this book, you are and always will be, a friend for all seasons.

Zack, The Palace Pussycat. It's not easy to motivate a cat to put his thoughts down on paper. Once he got started he worked doggedly without a peep until he was satisfied with his work.

Brenda Copeland, my incredible editor. With me from the first word keeping Zack and I on track, motivating, sympathizing and lending moral support, a shoulder and a hug, while using a gentle editorial pencil.

Thanks

All of you at Pocket Books who make it happen, Judith, Karen, Tracy, Seale, Cathy Lee, Craig and Barry.

Nigel Stoneman, my rocket from Pocket, UK.

Win and Carolyn Holden, Alan and Debbie Centofante, Beth McDonald, Bill Austin, Christi Paul, Jim Ranaldo, Brian Gilbert, Lisa and Bobby Aguilar, and Mark Manley, you make being Queen a pleasure.

Chester, Spanky, Max, Peke-A-Boo, Phoenix, See-Aye-Tee, and Bubba for conferring with Zack.

Chris and Brian Centofante. May God always smile on you and keep you safe.

To all of you, remember, if I can be Queen you can be anything you want—it's never too late!

The Year Ahead

I've been at this cleaning business a long time, and still I'm surprised by the number of people who get hung up on what to clean and when. Seems that for some people, cleaning is a dirty word. They want to know how often to clean this, when to put away that—as if there's going to be a big test at the end of the cleaning semester. But life's not like that. Sometimes you win. Sometimes you lose. Sometimes your house is clean. Sometimes . . . well, let's just leave it at that, shall we?

I don't believe in keeping to someone else's schedule and someone else's rules. I believe in making my schedule work for me, and I have only one rule: IF IT'S NOT DIRTY, DON'T CLEAN IT. We're all busy, and we all have better things to do than clean house. No one but the marines wears white gloves these days, so we don't have to be concerned with the white glove test. That said, few of us are happy living in a home that's dirty or unkempt. It's hard to relax when the dust bunnies are having a rodeo in the corner of your living room.

Sit back and think for a moment. What does clean mean for you? How organized do you want to be? Are you the type of person who's just dying to rearrange the magazines at the dentist's office, the one your office mate runs to when she spills cola on her keyboard? Or are you the person whose idea of cleaning is to put the dirty dishes in the oven, whose laundry schedule is determined by *Can I get away with this another day?*

Chances are you won't have to think too much about this. You already know who you are. You know what makes you comfortable and how you like to live. I suspect that despite our natural tendencies, most of us flit between one group and another. There are times when we feel that things are ordered and under control, just as there are times when chaos rules. I'm not trying to get you to change teams, to convert you or give you a cleaning citation. I want you to find your comfort, to do the things that will get you there, and help you stay there.

And that's where this book comes in. I've started off with a list of things to think about, from everyday household tasks that you'd never overlook (like washing dishes) to those uncommon tasks and easy oversights, such as flipping your mattress and cleaning the gutters. I'd like to encourage you to find out what's right for you. Some people, for example, may like to change their sheets every week. Others may find every two weeks often enough for them. A schedule only works if it's flexible and realistic. Start with that in mind and you can't go wrong.

That's part of what this book is about. Establishing a routine that works for you. The other part? Fun stuff. Each month brings its own particular signature. February, for example, can be a time of high heating bills, but it's also a time for Valentine's Day and romance, and that can mean flowers, champagne and chocolates (for starters . . .). I'll let you in on the best ways to care for flowers, how to help keep the bubble in that bottle of champers, and what to do when the chocolate strays on to the furniture and bed linen. (Oh, don't tell me you've never eaten chocolate in bed!) Turn to April, and you'll find some fun, natural ways to color your Easter eggs, as well as how to get ready for allergy season. October contains some Halloween fun, and December, as you might imagine, rounds out the year with lots of holiday advice.

But that's not all. I've included a few recipes throughout the book (well . . . you *have* been asking), and I'm also including some recommendations from my four-legged co-writer: Zack The Palace Pussycat. Zack helped me with my last two books (mainly by sitting on the manuscript), and this time he wanted to contribute further, so look for his suggestions in THE CAT'S MEOW. Zack's segments provide advice from the feline point of view, and of course he reminds us that behind every successful woman there's usually a rather talented cat.

This is not your typical cleaning book. But then again, I'm not your typical Queen!

It's About Time

DAILY DUTIES

Personally, there are only two things that I do *every* day: kiss the King and feed the cat. I make the bed most days (it's so much nicer to come home to), and I do try to see that the dishes are done, but sometimes I'm just so busy or distracted that even the simplest tasks fall by the wayside.

We're all very busy. We all have too much to do. That's why I've kept this list of daily chores short. Carry out these few tasks on most days and you'll find your life running smoother than you could imagine. Miss a day . . . well, the dishes will still be there tomorrow.

- Make beds.
- Put dirty clothes in the hamper.
- Hang up clothes.
- Clean up spills.
- Wash dishes.
- Wipe counters and stovetop.

TWICE WEEKLY

I've kept this list gloriously short—only one item:

- Vacuum carpets!

You can get away with vacuuming carpets just once a week (six days is the average gestation period for dust bunnies), but vacuuming twice weekly will prevent the dirt from getting ground into the fibers, and will therefore prolong the life of the carpet.

WEEKLY

Weekends were made for more than housework, so try spreading these tasks out through the week if you can.

- Sweep hardwood floors.
- Dust hard furniture.
- Dust knickknacks.

- Do the laundry.
- Change sheets.
- Clean sinks.
- Clean showers and tubs.
- Clean the toilet.
- Clean bathroom mirrors.
- Empty trash cans, put out garbage. (Clean the trash can if odors remain.)
- Sweep porch, patio and doormats.

BIWEEKLY

- Vacuum stairs.
- Dust TV/VCR/stereos, etc.

MONTHLY

- Replace the bag on your vacuum.
- Vacuum upholstery.
- Clean makeup brushes and sponges.
- Clean hairbrushes and combs.
- Vacuum drapes.
- Clean mirrors.
- Vacuum or dust blinds and shutters.
- Dust ceiling fans.
- Dust woodwork and dust down any cobwebs.
- Wash kitchen and bathroom area rugs.
- Vacuum carpet edges.

- Check hard floors and re-wax heavy traffic areas if needed.
- Clean out the refrigerator.
- Spot clean the kitchen cabinet fronts.
- Clean the fronts of stove, refrigerator, dishwasher, etc.
- Check the furnace filter: change or clean if needed.
- Hose off entry mats.
- Sweep out the garage.

QUARTERLY

- Sweep or wash the walkways and driveways.
- Change or clean the furnace filter.
- Wipe off lightbulbs as you dust (be sure they are cool).
- Look over knickknacks and wash or thoroughly clean any that require more than dusting.
- Flip the cushions on chairs and sofas for even wear.
- Clean humidifiers and dehumidifiers.

TWICE A YEAR

- It's got to be done: clean the oven.
- Clean stove hood and/or exhaust fan.
- Check the contents of freezer for things that are past their freshness. Clean freezer.
- Turn the mattresses on beds.
- Wash any plastic, vinyl or leather furniture.
- Clean scatter rugs.

- Dust books on shelves, making sure to dust shelves under the books.
- Vacuum the heat registers and cold air returns.
- Vacuum under furniture.
- Check silverware and clean if necessary.
- Replace that little box of baking soda in the refrigerator.
- Dust all the things you haven't been able to reach all year long.
- Clean bedspreads and slipcovers.
- Clean closets as you change seasonal clothes.

ANNUALLY

- Wash blankets and comforters.
- Dust down walls.
- Wash walls (every two years).
- Strip any waxed floors and re-wax.
- Wash all windows and screens.
- Wash or dry-clean drapery.
- Move and clean under and behind large items.
- Wash blinds.
- Clean carpet and upholstery.
- Clean any areas you have avoided all year long.
- Have the air conditioner checked and cleaned.
- Have the furnace checked and cleaned.
- Sort through the medicine cabinet, clean it, and organize and discard old medicine.

- Clean out kitchen cupboards, wash and reorganize.
- Replace the batteries in smoke detectors and other safety devices.
- Check the batteries in flashlights.
- Clean rain gutters.
- Wash all exterior windows.
- If you have a chimney, clean it.

So there you have it. Your annual checklist. Now read on for some fun stuff.

A Queen
for All
Seasons

✦☙ January ☙✦

It's January, a time of good intentions and new beginnings. We've made our resolutions and, with any luck, have recovered from our seasonal indulgences. We're ready for a fresh start. But first we have to clean up from last year. That means putting away the Christmas decorations and taking down the tree, storing the lights, and all that half-price wrapping paper that seemed like such a good idea at the time. So let's get to it. If we start now, we'll still have time to enjoy that Super Bowl party!

Let's Un-Deck the Halls

Putting up decorations can be a lot of fun, what with all the excitement of the holidays to look forward to. But there are few surprises after Christmas—unless, of course, you're talking about that mystery stain you've just discovered on the hall carpet. The best way to clean up after the holidays is to take a deep breath, roll up your sleeves, and get down to it. The sooner you start, the sooner you'll be finished. And isn't that what it's all about?

LIGHTS

If you just whip the lights off of the house and tree and toss them in a box, you'll hate yourself come next December when you find them twisted, tangled and broken. Wrap them around an empty paper roll instead. Take a large paper roll—one from wrapping paper will do fine—and cut a notch at one end. Tuck one end of the lights in the notch and start rolling them around the tube. When you get to the end of the tube make another notch to fasten that end of the lights. Do this to each strand, clearly labeling the tubes as you go—indoor or outdoor lights, tree lights or decorative strands, etc. Make sure you separate any lights that aren't functioning properly and mark those too, either for repair or scavenging.

Large lights or extra long lengths can be rolled in a circle, like a cowboy loops a rope. Delicate, expensive or special light strands can be stored in the type of inexpensive plastic food bowls that come with covers. The lights won't get crushed or broken, and they can be stacked for storage without damage.

CHRISTMAS TREES

Taking down the tree is really a two-person job, so try to enlist some help. A tree bag is your best bet, as it will prevent pine needles from being trailed through the house. Just make sure to buy a bag large enough to cover the base of the tree, and long enough to cover the height. The first step is to siphon off all the water that you can—a turkey baster works great. Next, lay a large covering, such as a plastic shower curtain, on the floor. Take a good look around to ensure that breakables are safe, and make sure you're well out of range of any hanging light fixtures. Loosen the tree stand, and gently tip the tree onto the covering, being careful not to shed too many needles or spill any remaining water left in the reservoir. (Remember the first rule of cleaning: If you don't make a mess, you won't have to clean it up!) Don't pull the bag up haphazardly, and don't tug. Be gentle and gradually unroll the bag up the length of the tree, something like putting on a pair of panty hose. (If you wear panty hose, that is . . .) Once you've got the tree into the bag, tie it tightly and drag it outside. You can, of course, carry the tree, but there's always the chance that you'll drop it, and that may cause damage.

Artificial trees can be stored fully assembled in Christmas tree storage bags. Simply open the bag, "fold" up the limbs on the tree as directed (You did keep the booklet that came with the tree, didn't you?), place the tree carefully into the bag and zip it up! Lack of storage space may dictate that you dismantle the tree and keep it in a box. If that's the case, just make sure to identify the branches, base and stem—unless, of course, you like jigsaw puzzles.

ORNAMENTS

First, make sure to dust the ornaments before you store them. Used fabric softener sheets are great for this job, but you will need rather a lot. Wipe the ornament with the used dryer sheet, then cover it so that the *other* side of the sheet touches the ornament. The fabric softener sheet will protect the ornament during storage, and the residue of softener will help to repel static electricity—and therefore, dust—when you hang it on the tree next year! Once you've wrapped the ornament, place it gently in a storage container, such as a shoe box or plastic storage carton. Those large metal canisters that once held popcorn are great, too.

Did you know?

Decorative candles can be cleaned quite easily with a cotton ball moistened with rubbing alcohol.

Whatever container you use, make sure not to overcrowd it or force the lid down, and try not to use tape to secure the box. Tape can ruin the box for future use and, if stored in an attic, can get sticky and gummy during the hot summer months. That can cause a real mess. A bungee cord hooked around the ends of the container will keep the lid firmly closed. Try that instead.

Once again, make sure to mark the storage container, and make sure to separate ornaments that are expensive or have sentimental value. Delicate elongated ornaments can be stored inside a toilet paper tube, and smaller items can be placed safely in egg cartons. Save silk balls that are starting to unravel by giving them a spritz with some hair spray or spray starch.

WRAPPING PAPER

The most important thing about storing Christmas paper is to actually remember that you have it so you don't go out and buy more next year! Either put the paper in an obvious spot so that it's the first thing you see as you start to take out the decorations, or make a note that you have *x* number of rolls on hand. It's not a bargain if you buy it twice!

I store my wrapping paper under the bed. Long plastic storage containers meant for this purpose work exceptionally well, and can be found quite inexpensively in dollar and discount stores. If you don't have a storage container, lay the rolls of paper on the floor and tie them together with some string or an elastic band. A bungee cord hooked into the ends of the rolls will hold the paper in a neat bundle. Just make sure to slip them into a large garbage bag to keep them clean during storage. Some people like to store their wrapping paper and ribbons in an old suitcase. That can work well, just as long as you remember which one you've used. You don't want to end up in the Bahamas with nothing to wear but Santa Claus wrapping paper and a big red bow! As I've said, labeling is important.

RIBBONS AND BOWS

• Store pre-made bows in a plastic storage or shoe box to prevent them from getting scrunched up. If you've bought an assortment of bows, tip them out of the bag and into the box. Those bags always seem to be too small to hold the bows, and so many of them wind up flattened and bent.

I hate it when that happens . . .

You've just found the perfect color bow at the bottom of the bag and, darn, if it isn't crushed! Not to worry. Crushed bows can be brought back to life by putting them in the dryer on air fluff (no heat) for a few short minutes. Presto! Good as new.

• Keep rolls of ribbon tidy by putting a rubber band or ponytail holder around the roll. You'll prevent unraveling that way.

BOBBLES, BANGLES AND BEADS— IN OTHER WORDS, *MISCELLANEOUS!*

• Garland is usually too lush to be wrapped around just one paper roll, so fasten a few tubes together with a rubber band and wind the garland around that. Make sure you wrap the garland around the roll like a candy cane, side-to-side, and secure it in notches that you've cut in each end. Don't draw the garland from top to bottom—the strand could stretch or break.

• Dust silk flowers before storing them with a blow-dryer, set on cool.

• If you store Christmas dishes in plastic wrap or stacked in Ziploc™ bags you won't have to wash them before using next year.

• Make sure to launder Christmas tablecloths and napkins prior to storing. Old spills will oxidize during storage and can be difficult, if not impossible, to remove.

Save those empty baby wipe boxes. They come in handy for storing gift tags and those slivers of ribbon that are so handy for decorating small packages.

• Take care when storing the Nativity scene. Wrap each figure separately, either in tissue paper or a used fabric softener sheet. Paper towels don't work well for this job because their fibers can catch on any rough edges. If you do scratch a figurine, try touching it up with a child's colored pencil.

Delicate Christmas knickknacks can be stored in egg cartons.

• Artificial wreaths can be stored year-to-year in a large pillowcase (depending on the size of the wreath) or in a large plastic bag. Wrap some tissue paper around the wreath first, but be gentle when removing it—you don't want to damage any of the branches. If the ribbon on the wreath is flattened, just plump it up with a curling iron.

• Many charities make good use of discarded Christmas cards. St. Jude's Ranch, for example, is a nonprofit youth home that teaches kids a trade and a way to earn money by cutting off the verse and making the fronts into new cards. Entire cards are welcome, as are cards with the backs cut off. For more information call 1-800-492-3562, or visit St. Jude's website at www.stjudesranch.org.

MAKING A LIST, CHECKING IT TWICE

Make a note of what seasonal items you've stored, and *where* you've put them. If you make a list of what you think you'll need next year—wrapping paper, Christmas cards, extension cords, larger-sized pants—you'll be in a good position to pick up bargains. More importantly, you'll save yourself that last-minute flurry of panic when you realize that your tree lights don't reach the outlet. Remember: Excitement is good. Panic is bad.

It's Time for That Super Bowl Party!

I love Super Bowl parties. Everybody seems to be in such great spirits. Good friends, good food, and good fun. What could be better?

TOUCH-UPS AFTER TOUCHDOWNS

You wouldn't cry over spilt milk, so why shed a tear over beer? First thing to do for a beer spill on the carpet is to blot up all the liquid you can, then flush the area with club soda and blot, blot, blot again. Now turn to a great carpet spotter like Spot Shot Instant Carpet Stain Remover® and follow the directions carefully. Try to avoid carpet cleaners that contain stain repellents. If the beer doesn't come out during the first try, the repellent could lock in the stain and you could be left with a permanent mark.

Beer stains on clothes? Flush with cool water, work in a few drops of liquid dishwashing soap and launder as usual.

Salsa—the sauce, not the dance—tastes so good and stains so bad. For salsa spills, blot with club soda as soon as possible, then treat with Wine Away Red Wine Stain Remover™ or Red Erase®. Both are fabulous at removing red stains from carpets, upholstery *and* clothes.

Guacamole is my favorite, but what a cleaning disaster it is! Think about it: It's oily *and* green. Clean up guacamole spills on carpets and upholstery by scraping with a dull, straight edge, such as a credit card. (The one you used to pay for the party should do nicely.) Remove as much *gunk* as possible, then flush with club soda and blot, blot, blot! Let sit 10 minutes, then flush with cool, clear water. Once the surface is dry, apply a good carpet and upholstery cleaner according to the directions on the container. If you still have a green reminder, mix up a solution of ½ cup of hydrogen peroxide and 1 teaspoon of ammonia, spray on liberally, let sit 15 minutes, then blot. Continue until the stain is removed and then flush with club soda and blot until you have removed all the moisture possible.

If you happen to be wearing the guacamole stain, treat with Zout® Stain Remover or rubbing alcohol. Gently dab the alcohol on the stain and let sit for 15 minutes before pre-treating and laundering as usual.

If your house has that smoky, day-after smell, bring some white vinegar to a boil, then reduce to a simmer for about 30 minutes, being careful not to let the pan boil dry. Let the vinegar stand and after a few hours unwanted odors will be absorbed.

Did you know?

Simmering orange or lemon peels can give your home a fresh, natural scent.

If the upholstery smells like smoke, lay a clean sheet on the furniture and sprinkle it with ODORZOUT™. Let sit overnight, then remove the sheet and shake outside. ODORZOUT™ is all natural and won't hurt anything. For carpet odors, sprinkle directly, then vacuum in the morning.

Spilled ashtray? Don't reach for the vacuum—at least not right away. You could have a nasty vacuum fire on your hands, at which point you'll be wishing that a spilled ashtray was your only problem! Pick up any butts and dispose of them in an empty can until you are sure they are cool. Ash on hard floors should be cleaned with a broom and dustpan; ash on carpet should be vacuumed using only the hose—no beater bar, which could grind the ash into the carpet. If you're sensitive to cigarette odors, you may want to dispose of the vacuum bag or empty the canister. Never apply water to an ashtray spill. You'll have a black, gooey mess on your hands that's far worse than anything you started with.

Somebody break a glass? It's bound to happen. Pick up the large shards first, then use a cut potato to pick up the slivers. (Yes, a potato.) Just cut the potato in half and press down on the glass with the damp side. Vacuum the remaining small pieces, using the attachment hose to concentrate the suction, then vacuum the carpet thoroughly. Never use a vacuum with a beater bar to vacuum glass until you've picked up all you can with the potato and the attachment hose. The beater bar will only flip the glass around, making it harder to clean up the debris.

Let's Dish!

Guacamole is such a wonderful Super Bowl tradition. And now that you know how to clean it up, you can serve it with flair! Here's my favorite recipe:

Chi Chi's Super Bowl Guacamole

4 ripe avocados, mashed or pureed (can do in food processor)

½ cup canned diced green chilies

¼ cup minced onion

1 tablespoon salt

¼ cup lemon juice

Combine all ingredients, cover and chill. Serve with corn chips. Makes about 3 cups.

❤❤ February ❤❤

This is the month of cold weather and high heating bills. Thank goodness it's also the month of love. Offset the winter cold by snuggling with your honey. Let those Valentine's flowers remind you of spring, and brighten those long winter nights with some sparkling jewelry. And if Cupid does leave his mark, well, look no further for some quick cleanup tips.

Conservation for the Nation

Cuddling is an energy-efficient way to keep warm. Want to save water? Bathe with a friend! Of course there are other ways to save on your energy bill.

• Why heat an empty house? Lower the thermostat when your family is out during the day—try 65 degrees or so—and bring the heat back up in the evening. If you lower the temperature when everybody is toasty warm in bed, you'll cut your bill even further. A double setback thermostat can adjust the temperature according to your needs. It's well worth the money.

• Moist air retains heat, so invest in a humidifier (or adapt your existing heating system) and you could lower your thermostat by another 3 or 4 degrees. That can save you up to 12 percent on your heating bill!

• A gas-fired heating system should be professionally cleaned and serviced at least once a year to keep it working at maximum efficiency. Oil-fired systems should be cleaned and serviced twice a year. Those of you who have had the misfortune of a furnace backup *know* I'm giving you good advice. Cleaner is better.

• Shut the dishwasher off at the dry cycle and allow dishes to air-dry with the door partially open.

• Just cooked a nice roast dinner? Leave the door open a crack (once you've turned off the oven, that is), and let the heat warm the room as the oven cools. Don't do this if you have young children—nothing is worth a potential burn.

• Keep radiators, registers and ducts clean. Vacuum with the duster brush attachment; for hard to reach spots use a telescoping duster. Make sure they're clear of debris and free from obstructions, such as furniture and draperies.

• Replace furnace filters frequently. A clean filter will distribute heat more efficiently. Check filters monthly, say the first of every month. Vacuum to remove dust, and replace filters when vacuuming alone won't get the filter clean. Disposable filters should be replaced at least every three months.

• Heat can escape through air conditioners, so store yours if you can. If that's not possible, do your best to winterize the unit. Cover the outside of the a/c with cardboard cut to size, and then wrap it in a heavy-duty plastic. Drop cloths and plastic tablecloths are ideal. Secure the covering with a bungee cord, making sure to avoid corner flaps that might tear in the wind.

• Conserve energy in winter *and* summer by adjusting the rotation on your ceiling fan. A counterclockwise rotation will push the hot air from the ceiling down into the room—perfect for winter. A clockwise rotation will pull up warm summer air and replace it with a nice, cool flow.

• Conserve water by taking showers instead of baths. The average bath uses 25 gallons of water, whereas the average shower uses just 10 gallons.

• Don't leave water running while you brush your teeth. Turn it off until you're ready to rinse.

That "small load" setting may save water, but the washing machine still goes through the same number of rotations. Avoid washing small loads if you can.

• Whenever possible, use cold or warm water for washing clothes. Always use cold water to rinse.

• Clean the lint filter on your clothes dryer each time you dry a load. Clothes will dry faster and more efficiently.

• That little black dress may be a hot number, but there's no reason to keep it warm. Keep closet doors closed.

Happy Valentine's Day!

Flowers, jewelry, candy? I'd love Valentine's Day even if it *wasn't* the day the King proposed!

PETAL PUSHERS

• Do your best to select the freshest flowers available. Look for healthy stems with unblemished leaves and petals. Flowers that are just beginning to bud will last longer than those in full bloom.

• Be sure to remove leaves that fall below the waterline. They can contaminate the water.

• Cut stems on an angle while holding them under running water, then immerse in fresh water. It's best to do this in the early morning when it's coolest.

• Coarse, heavy stems (you'll find them on flowers such as gladiolus, mums, pussy willows, forsythia, and even roses) should be split with a sharp knife before placing in water. This will encourage the stem to drink up the water. Pounding the base of the stem with a wooden spoon works well, too.

• Change the water every day. And for a longer life, add one of the following mixtures:

A teaspoon of sugar and about a ¼ teaspoon of lemon juice

Several aspirin tablets that have been dissolved in a little warm water

A tablespoon of liquid bleach. That will stop the water from clouding; particularly useful when using a clear vase.

• Prolong the life of flowers by keeping them cool and displaying them out of direct sunlight.

• Remove anthers from lilies. Those long, pollen-bearing shoots can rub off on clothes, carpeting and walls and can be extremely difficult to remove.

Clean pollen stains from clothing by sponging with rubbing alcohol. Don't use anything with ammonia. That will set the stain.

ARTFUL ARRANGEMENTS

• Flowers too short for the vase? Place stems in plastic drinking straws before arranging.

• Vase too deep? Fill it with marbles prior to adding water and flowers.

• Wilted flowers? Snip about an inch off the ends and stand them in hot water for about 20 to 30 minutes before returning to a vase of clean, cool water.

• Make sure floral foam is saturated with water before adding flowers.

• Arrange large flowers first, then follow with smaller blossoms and greenery.

Did you know?
Tulips are the only flowers that continue to grow after they've been cut!

• Coffeepots, teapots and milk bottles make lovely imaginative vases.

• Plastic hair rollers are great for arranging flowers. Stand them upright in the bottom of the vase and place stems in the cylinders to keep them in position.

• Try to match the flowers to the vase. Hourglass shapes are good for single-bloom flowers like tulips, and urns are great for flowers that droop easily. Slim, cylindrical vases are best for tall flowers like gladiolus.

• Placing your arrangement in front of a mirror will double the impact of your flowers.

DIAMONDS ARE A GIRL'S BEST FRIEND

Who doesn't love to get a gift of jewelry? Who doesn't know how to care for it?

• Rubbing alcohol is great for cleaning costume jewelry. Pour a little rubbing alcohol over the piece—place the jewelry in a shallow dish or small container first—and gently brush with a soft toothbrush. A word of caution: Many costume pieces are glued, and soaking can loosen the glue. Try not to saturate. Finish with a quick rinse in cool water and wipe dry.

• Costume jewelry that doesn't contain glue can be cleaned with denture-cleaning tablets. Drop a few tablets in a cup of warm water and allow the jewelry to soak for 5 minutes or so. Rinse and dry well. For intricate pieces, dry with a blow-dryer.

• Remove dirt from intricate pieces by brushing with a soft bristle toothbrush and some white, nongel toothpaste.

Rinse by brushing with a clean toothbrush and just water, and dry well.

Restore the luster to pearls by buffing gently with a soft cloth moistened with olive oil.

• Clean diamonds by placing in a tea strainer and dipping them in a pot of boiling water into which you have added several drops of ammonia and a drop or two of dishwashing liquid. Immerse for a few short seconds and then rinse in cold water. For extra sparkle, dip the diamonds in a little bit of undiluted vodka or alcohol for a minute or two, then rinse and pat dry. This may be used for hard stones such as diamonds, rubies and sapphires. *Do not* use this method on emeralds.

• Emeralds are extremely soft. They can crack easily and absorb water, so buff them with a soft toothbrush or an ACT Natural™ Microfiber Cloth. Don't soak them or immerse them in water, and if you want a thorough cleaning, take them to a professional.

• Remove tarnish from silver with a paste of lemon juice and baking soda. Apply the mixture with a soft toothbrush, then allow to dry. Remove with a clean, dry toothbrush and polish with a clean, soft cloth.

• Jade can be washed in mild, soapy water. Dry immediately.

• Opals and turquoise are porous stones that should not be washed. Brush settings with a dry, soft toothbrush and shine with chamois-type leather or an ACT Natural™ Microfiber Cloth.

• Wash gold in a bowl of soapy water. A soft, gentle stroke with a soft toothbrush will help clean crevices, details and links. Dry with a soft, lint-free towel and then buff with a chamois or microfiber cloth.

> **I hate it when that happens . . .**
>
> *Tangled chains got you in knots? Place a drop of baby oil on the chain, then gently untangle by pulling the links apart with two sewing needles.*

• Always fasten a chain-link necklace before storing to prevent tangles. Chains that tangle easily can be slipped through a drinking straw. Cut the straw to half the length of the chain, drop the chain through and fasten the clasp on the outside of the straw. No more tangles.

The Valentine's Day Stain Chain

Love should last forever, not that chocolate stain.

• Chocolate on clothes requires special treatment. Scrape off all you can with a dull straight edge, taking care not to force the chocolate more deeply into the fabric. Gently apply some Zout® Stain Remover, allow it to sit on the fabric 5 minutes or so (don't let it dry), and then flush under a forceful stream of warm water. If a grease mark is still visible, sponge with any good dry-cleaning solution such as Engergine Cleaning Fluid®. For really tough stains, soak in Brilliant Bleach® by Soapworks. Follow package directions carefully.

• Chocolate on carpets should be treated immediately with your favorite carpet cleaner. Try Spot Shot Carpet Stain Remover®. For really stubborn stains, saturate the area with ½ cup of hydrogen peroxide, to which you have added 1 teaspoon of ammonia. Allow to sit for 20 minutes, then blot. You may need to repeat this process. Once the stain is gone, flush the area with club soda and blot by standing on old heavy towels. This should remove the moisture. Allow to fully dry before walking on the area.

You can keep the fizz in champagne for hours if you slip the handle of a metal teaspoon down the neck of the bottle. I don't know why it works, but it does!

• Champagne spills should be sponged immediately with club soda. The salt in the soda will help to prevent permanent stains and the carbonation will draw the spill from the fibers. Two remedies for the price of one!

• Dried alcohol stains will turn brown as they age, so quick removal is important.

• Champagne spills on clothes should first be blotted with club soda, then pre-treated with a good laundry stain remover.

• Champagne spills on carpets should be treated with Spot Shot Instant Carpet Stain Remover®. Just make sure to blot well with club soda first. Treat spills on upholstery the same way, drying with a hair dryer to prevent a ring from forming.

• Stains from pink champagne can be removed with Wine Away Red Wine Stain Remover®.

• Perfume stains can be avoided if you apply your fragrance *before* you get dressed. Make sure it's dry before putting on your clothes.

• Perfume is a combination of alcohol and oil—deadly to fabrics. Treat perfume stains with Zout® Stain Remover and launder as soon as possible. If the fabric is dry-clean only, be sure to point out the stain to your dry cleaner.

• Never iron an area that has been sprayed with perfume. You might set the stain, or worse, remove the color from the fabric!

• Perfume stains can be removed from sturdy fabrics with a lather of Fels-Naptha Soap® and warm water. Work well into the stain, let sit 15 minutes and launder as usual.

• Stains from massage oil can be removed with a good waterless hand cleaner, such as GOJO™. Rub it well into the fabric—*massage* it in if you'd like!—then flush with warm water. A paste of liquid dish soap and 20 Mule Team® Borax will also work. Launder as usual using your normal detergent and the hottest possible water for the fabric. One-half cup of 20 Mule Team® Borax will ensure that all residue is removed.

• Oil stains on carpets should be covered quickly with baking soda. Allow the baking soda to absorb the oil—this may take several hours—then vacuum it up using the attachment hose to concentrate the suction. Vacuum very well with the hose before vacuuming with a beater bar to remove all of the baking soda. Finish off with your favorite carpet cleaner.

March

It's spring! The flowers are blooming, the birds are singing, everything's fresh and new, and you can't wait to get started with your spring-cleaning. Yikes! Did I say spring-cleaning? That has no part in my spring fantasy. How about yours? Spring-cleaning was a necessity a long time ago when log cabins were boarded up to keep out the winter cold. The arrival of spring presented the first opportunity to clean out all the soot and grime that had accumulated during the long winter months—hence the term spring-cleaning. Those of you living in log cabins may want to continue this practice, but for the rest of us, well, there are better things to do.

That's not to say that there aren't certain times of the year when you'll want to clean a little more thoroughly. It may be just after Christmas, it may be right before Aunt Martha's next visit . . . it might even be spring. *When* you do it is entirely up to you. As for *what* to do, read on.

Spring Forward

DON'T CLEAN YOUR CLUTTER

The hardest part of cleaning is working around the accumulation of all those things you've somehow acquired. If you really want to streamline your cleaning process, take a few minutes, go room to room and take stock of what's in sight, as well as what's hiding in your cupboards. I'll bet my crown (the cheap cardboard one . . .) that you have things that haven't been used in three, five, ten years or more. Think carefully. Do you really want to keep that purple giraffe? Do you really want to clean it?

If you can't bear to part with your collectibles (I love cats and pigs—don't ask), consider storing some and displaying others, rotating your selection from time to time. You'll have less to clean.

If you have a lot of treasures, think about investing in a glass-fronted display cabinet. The glass will protect your ornaments from dust, and you shouldn't have to clean them more than once a year.

Are you really going to read all those back issues of *National Geographic*? Don't be timid. Throw them out.

If that cat figurine that Aunt Lucille gave you 10 years ago is missing a paw and part of its tail, look at it, smile at the memories and then say good-bye. Don't keep things that are broken and can't be repaired.

Think before you purchase the latest gadget. If you don't buy it, you won't have to clean it.

A WORD ABOUT CLEANING PRODUCTS

Gather all your cleaning products together in one container before you start your rounds—something with a handle is ideal. If you have more than one bathroom, think about purchasing a set of cleaning products for each. It may cost more at the time, but you'll save yourself the aggravation of toting products from one floor to the next.

Can't find any twist ties and the trash bag is full? Just use dental floss or a rubber band. Both are tough and water resistant, so you don't have to worry about the rain.

Make sure you have plenty of clean cloths and vacuum bags. If you anticipate throwing out a lot of garbage, make sure you have lots of good, strong bags. Check supplies of soaps and any all-purpose cleaners that you may use. There's nothing worse than starting a task only to have to stop halfway because you don't have what you need at hand.

The most expensive products are not always the best. Try store brands and homemade solutions—they can work just as well as their more expensive counterparts.

Try not to depend on harsh chemicals. Things like baking soda, white vinegar, 20 Mule Team® Borax, Fels-Naptha Soap®, lemon juice, salt and club soda work just as well and aren't harmful to your family or the environment. Baking soda is a great deodorizer and a wonderfully mild abrasive. White vinegar is a terrific cleaner, especially for soap scum and mildew. Borax is a never-be-without laundry additive, and Fels-Naptha Soap® is great for stubborn stains. And let's not forget the club soda, lemon juice and salt. Club soda works on all sorts of spills; lemon juice is a great natural bleach; and salt can be used on just about everything, from artificial flowers to clogged drains.

Be wary of using too many antibacterial products. Unless you're prepping for surgery, good old soap and water work just fine.

Look for odor eliminators instead of cover-ups. Make sure to purchase products without scent. Try using baking soda or a good, natural odor eliminator such as ODORZOUT™.

Don't forget to change that little box of baking soda in your fridge. Pour the old box down the drain, and chase it with a ½ cup of white vinegar, and you'll create a little volcano to naturally clean and freshen drains.

Smells in old trunks and drawers can be eliminated with a slice of white bread placed in a bowl and covered with white vinegar. Close the trunk or drawer for 24 hours, and when you remove the bread and vinegar the odor will be gone!

Fresh, dry coffee grounds will remove smells from refrigerators.

A pan of cat litter will remove musty smells in closets and basements.

Place crumpled newspaper in drawers to remove musty odors.

Put dryer fabric softener sheets in luggage, storage containers, closets and drawers to leave a clean, fresh scent.

FIRST THINGS FIRST

Decide on your approach and be consistent. If you decide to clean for an hour, stick to it. If you decide to clean one room now and another tomorrow, stick to that. Indecision and distraction can really affect how well you clean. If you start out doing one thing and end up doing another, you'll have a houseful of half-finished projects, and you won't feel as if you've accomplished anything. That can be very frustrating, to say the least.

I like to start with the room that requires the least amount of effort, and that's generally the one that's used the least. It may be the guest room, the living room . . . it may even be the kitchen. Hey—no judgments. Think of it as a sort of warm-up. Start with the lightest task and you'll see results fast. That will motivate you to keep going!

Generally speaking, work from top to bottom. Dust from the light fixtures, tops of furniture, etc., will fall onto the carpet and floors. So do floors last and you'll know that your house really is clean.

Remember: If it isn't dirty, don't clean it!

Don't backtrack. Finish one task before moving to another. Put on some high-spirited music to set the pace and keep you going.

LET'S GET STARTED

Dusting comes first. But don't just pick up any old cloth, and don't, for heaven's sake, use a feather duster. They may be some man's fantasy, but they just scatter the dust all around. Really, they're worse than useless. I strongly recommend washable lambs wool dusters. Lambs wool both attracts and contains dust, so it won't whisk the dust around from one surface to the other. Lambs wool is also washable, so it lasts for years. (You can buy lambs wool dusters in many varieties, including dust mitts and telescoping dusters, which are great for those hard-to-reach corners.)

Use a telescoping lambs wool duster to clean ceiling fans.

Don't just move ornaments while you're dusting. Make sure to dust them, too!

After you've dusted your electronic equipment, it's a good idea to give it a wipe with some rubbing alcohol. Apply with a clean, soft cloth, then buff dry. Make sure to turn the power off first, though.

Once you've dusted, give the upholstery a good going-over. Use the appropriate attachment on your vacuum cleaner—the small brush for cushions and arms, the long nozzle for crevices and hard-to-reach areas. If you own a sofa bed, make sure to open it up and vacuum the mattress. (Most sofa bed mattresses are one-side only, so don't try to flip it.) Don't forget to vacuum scatter cushions.

Climb the walls, I mean *clean* the walls, by tying a towel over the head of a broom and pulling it down the wall. Shake out the towel as necessary, and change it when it becomes soiled. Work up and down the wall—not side to side—and use strokes that are comfortable for you. Complete one room at a time.

Walls don't need to be washed every year unless you're a smoker. So don't wash walls that don't need it. If, however, a room looks grimy, a good wall wash could save you the effort of painting.

FLOORS

Grit can scratch wood floors, so they should be swept before washing. Use long, directed strokes, moving from the corners to the center of the room. Sweep all the grit— that means crumbs, cat litter, and all that unidentifiable stuff—into a dustpan.

Now you're ready to wash with your favorite, gentle floor cleaner. Don't have a favorite wood floor cleaner? Try tea! The tannic acid gives the floor a wonderful shine. Use several tea bags to brew a quart or two. You can have a cup if you like, but let the rest cool to room temperature before using. Wring a soft cloth out in the tea. Make sure the cloth is damp, not wet. Overwetting the floor could warp it or damage the finish. Just in case I haven't been clear on this: *Yes, I am suggesting that you get down on your hands and knees.* Sorry, but anything else is just a shortcut, and if you want to clean your floors thoroughly, this is the only way to go.

• Start at the edges and move your hand across the floor, using a small circular motion.

• Keep the cloth well rinsed and continue until the entire floor is done.

• For vinyl or tile floors use the same cleaning method, substituting 1 gallon of warm water combined with 2 tablespoons of 20 Mule Team® Borax for the tea.

• For marble floors try the ACT Natural™ Microfiber

Mop. It uses nothing but water and thousands of little scrubbing fingers that pick up the dirt without scratching. It won't leave a film, either.

AND DON'T FORGET ...

• Give the inside of kitchen cupboards a wash with a simple solution of warm, soapy water. Anything sticky can be removed with a little baking soda.

• Grind some lemon rinds and ice cubes in the disposal to keep it clean and sharpen the blades, too.

• Vacuum your mattress with the upholstery attachment, then flip it for even wear. A plastic bag, such as a dry cleaner's bag, placed between the box spring and mattress will help ease the strain of this task. (Best not to take any chances, so if you have young children leave out the bag and let your muscles do the work.)

• Since you're flipping your mattress, don't forget to wash your mattress pad, blankets and pillows before putting the bed back together.

• Yes, even that self-cleaning oven needs to be cleaned.

• Draperies should be cleaned once a year. Please read the care label carefully and don't try to wash curtains that should be dry-cleaned.

You can extend the life of your window coverings by vacuuming them frequently.

• Not every room requires the same effort or attention, so decide before you begin what clean means to you.

• If you use the space under your bed for storage, remove the storage containers, vacuum the carpet and clean the containers before you put them back.

• If the woodwork on your walls is dirty, you should carefully wash it even though you do not wash the walls.

• Take down the globes from the overhead light fixtures, wash them and put them back up. While you're at it, when the lightbulbs are cool, dust them, too.

• If hinges are squeaking every time you open a door, lubricate them with a quick spray of silicone.

• Don't overlook door handles—wash and polish them. They get used constantly and seldom get washed.

Wearing of the Green Doesn't Have to Mean Grass Stains

Now that winter white is starting to disappear, just make sure that the greens of spring don't appear on your clothes!

Grass stains can be removed from clothing with the help of a little white, nongel toothpaste. Brush the toothpaste into the stain using an old, soft toothbrush—rinse and then launder. Zout® Stain Remover will also do the trick. Work a liberal amount into the fabric with your thumb and forefinger, then wash as usual.

Grass stains on jeans should be treated with rubbing alcohol. Saturate the stain, let sit for 10 to 15 minutes, then pop the jeans into the wash. Check to see that the stain has come out before you put the jeans into the dryer. Heat will set the stain and make it impossible to remove, so if you need to repeat the procedure, it's best to find out *before* you use the dryer.

For grass on white leather athletic shoes, try molasses. You heard me—*molasses!* Massage the stain with a dollop of molasses and let it sit overnight. Wash the shoes with soap and water the next morning, and the grass stains should come off along with the molasses.

Fabric shoes such as Keds® can be cleaned with baking soda. Dip a wet toothbrush into some baking soda and brush vigorously. Rinse well and dry out of the sun. No baking soda? Use white, nongel toothpaste instead.

If those blue suede shoes have had a meeting with the green, rub the stain with a nylon sponge that has been dipped in glycerin. Rub until the stain has been removed, then blot with a cloth dipped in undiluted white vinegar. Brush the nap to reset in the right direction, and allow the shoes to dry out of the sun.

Grass stains on carpets should be removed with a good quality carpet cleaner such as Spot Shot Instant Carpet Stain Remover®. Just follow the directions on the can. For stubborn stains, apply rubbing alcohol; wait 10 minutes, blot, then treat with your favorite carpet cleaner.

April

llergy season *and* tax time? If it weren't for Easter, April really would be the cruelest month. Don't fret. You can shorten the sneezin' season by allergy proofing your home. As far as taxes are concerned, well, I can't tell you how to pay less, but I can help with things like pencil marks and sweat stains. So turn your attention to Easter and the beauty of the month—those blue skies that remind us that the best things in life are free.

Spring Fever

The experts say that allergies are reactions to harmless substances that don't bother most people. Huh! If that's the case, why do so many people suffer from them? Seasonal allergies are caused by factors such as trees, grass and pollen. Year-round allergies are reactions to things like dust particles, animal dander, mold and dust mites. Whatever their cause, allergies can make us sneeze, sniff, cough and generally feel miserable—but you don't have to take it lying down.

CAN YOU DO WITHOUT IT?

Many detergents contain petroleum distillates—a major irritant for allergy sufferers. If freshly laundered clothes make you sneeze or itch, consider changing detergents. Be selective. Look for products marked "dye and perfume free," and check the label for colors or perfumes—you'll want to steer clear of them. I like PUREX®, a gentle detergent that does a great job on laundry. People with severe allergies or asthma may benefit from environmentally friendly products, such as those manufactured by Soapworks®. If you or anyone in your family suffers from allergies, you owe it to yourself to shop around.

Dryer fabric softener sheets can exacerbate allergies—best to do without them.

Allergy sufferers should use pump dispensers rather than aerosol sprays, which can fill the air with minute particles of irritants.

• If you must use hair spray, apply it outside the house so that the fumes won't linger.

• Look through your cleaning supplies and eliminate those with a strong scent, those loaded with chemicals, and those you've had for a long time. Products can undergo changes after time, and irritants can increase.

• Don't mix chemicals.

• Look for natural cleaning products such as baking soda, lemon juice, club soda, white vinegar, etc.

• Furniture polish can attract dust and dust mites. Best not to use it.

• Stuffed animals are huge dust collectors, so if your children have allergies, it's best to limit their exposure. Any cloth or fuzzy toy can be a potential allergy problem. If your child is having difficulties with allergies, remove toys one by one to determine those that can be tolerated—and those that can't.

Stuffed fabric toys that can't be washed can still be cleaned. Just place in a plastic bag with some baking soda and salt and shake vigorously a few times a day for several days. This should remove dust, dirt and odor.

FILTERS: NOT JUST FOR COFFEEMAKERS

• If there's a filter, clean it! This means vacuums, fans, air purifiers, etc.

• Change the furnace filter at least once a month or invest in one that can be washed. Make sure to wash it frequently.

• If your allergies are severe, consider wearing a filtration mask while vacuuming and dusting.

DON'T GET HAULED ON THE CARPET

• Dust and dander cling to carpets, so if you have severe allergies you may want to consider hard floors such as wood, laminate, and ceramics. These floors can be washed frequently and will do a lot to keep allergy symptoms at bay.

• If you have severe allergies but are unable to remove carpets, apply benzyl benzoate dry foam or 3 percent tannic acid, then vacuum using a cleaner with an effective filter system. Tannic acid breaks down mite allergens, and benzyl benzoate dry foam actually kills mites and helps remove them—and their waste products—from carpet.

Avoid placing houseplants directly on carpets and rugs. Moisture in the plant can cause condensation, and that in turn can cause mildew—a powerful irritant to allergy sufferers.

• Vacuuming can stir up dust mites and their droppings, so don't vacuum too frequently. Once a week is fine.

• Vacuum hard floors prior to mopping so that you don't stir up dust.

• Wash all hard floors with a quality cleaner created with allergy sufferers in mind. Try At Home All-Purpose Cleaner from Soapworks®.

• Damp-mop hard floors with a good quality mop that can be washed in the washing machine. Try the ACT Natural™ Microfiber Mop.

• Change the bag in your vacuum frequently. If you have a vacuum with a collection canister rather than a bag, empty it each time you vacuum.

SOFA, SO GOOD

• Stay away from fuzzy or flocked fabrics that are difficult to clean. Buy only upholstered pieces that can be cleaned with water.

• Vacuum upholstered pieces weekly.

• Stay clear of furniture with ruffles or fringes. They're notorious dust-catchers and notoriously difficult to clean.

• When shopping for upholstered furniture, look for pieces without loose pillows. Buy tailored pieces in tightly woven fabrics.

AND SO TO BED

• Sealing your bedroom door with weather-stripping will give you more control over your sleeping environment.

• Keep pets out of your bedroom.

• Something as innocent as wallpaper can cause mildew, so keep walls—especially bedroom walls—clear of papers and fabrics.

• Use an air purifier in your bedroom.

• Vacuum your mattress frequently. Invest in a good mattress cover—one that forms a protective cover but still allows the mattress to breathe.

• Wash all bedding in 130-degree water at least every 10 days. That includes blankets, pillows, comforters and mattress pads.

• If you can't wash pillows and comforters as frequently as you'd like, try placing them in the dryer on air fluff. That will help.

• Keep bedspreads, dust ruffles, decorator pillows, etc., dust free. Better yet, get rid of that dust ruffle.

• Stay away from down and feather pillows. They can aggravate allergies, even if you're *not* allergic to them. Use foam pillows encased in hypoallergenic covers that can be zipped shut.

AND DON'T FORGET ...

• Wash windows and screens frequently.

• Keep the house closed up as much as possible, especially on windy days.

• Plant flowers and trees that produce as little pollen as possible, such as ivy, African violets, and leafy plants such as philodendrons, piggyback plants, creeping pileas, and prayer plants.

• Install an air cleaner on the furnace or invest in a stand-alone air purifier.

• Don't keep fresh flowers indoors, no matter how beautiful.

• Keep your fireplace clean and make sure the damper is closed.

• Use natural lambs wool dusters. The lanolin traps the dust and keeps it from spreading.

• If you don't like to use lambs wool dusters, use a clean, damp cloth.

• Insects love stagnant water, so don't allow water to stand in fountains and plant bases.

• Remove dried flower arrangements. These dust catchers are very hard to keep clean.

• Invest in a dehumidifier and maintain it well. Empty it weekly and clean it, too. Wash it with a solution of 1 quart warm water and 2 teaspoons of chlorine bleach. Make sure you wipe down the coils, and pay special attention to the container that catches the water.

• Make sure your curtains are made of synthetic fiber. Natural fibers contain more lint and may aggravate allergies.

• Dust mites survive in dampness, so do everything in your power to keep the air dry—except moving to my house in Arizona!

• Keep cooking pots covered to eliminate steam.

• Use an exhaust fan over the stove when you cook.

• Don't hang clothes in the house to dry.

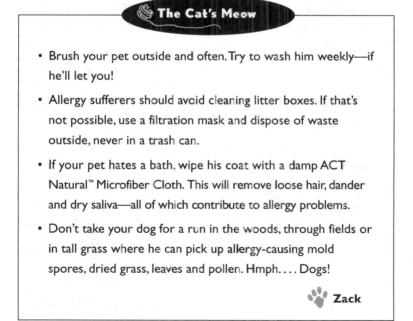

The Cat's Meow

• Brush your pet outside and often. Try to wash him weekly—if he'll let you!

• Allergy sufferers should avoid cleaning litter boxes. If that's not possible, use a filtration mask and dispose of waste outside, never in a trash can.

• If your pet hates a bath, wipe his coat with a damp ACT Natural™ Microfiber Cloth. This will remove loose hair, dander and dry saliva—all of which contribute to allergy problems.

• Don't take your dog for a run in the woods, through fields or in tall grass where he can pick up allergy-causing mold spores, dried grass, leaves and pollen. Hmph. . . . Dogs!

Zack

Taxing Times

Now that we've dealt with allergies, it's time to deal with those other seasonal irritants—taxes! Read on to find out how to deal with those stains and other little annoyances that come up at this time. Just think of me as your own personal support group!

No, I'm not going to tell you how to launder your money.

First, stock up on aspirin. You can use it to treat underarm stains, as well as that tax-season headache! (What do you mean you're not sweating?) For underarm stains on tee shirts and other cottons, dissolve 8 to 10 aspirin tablets to 1 cup of warm water, then saturate the underarm area of the garment. Allow to sit for 30 minutes and then launder as usual. If you're wearing the same tee night after night (hey, no judgments), rub the underarms with a bar of Fels-Naptha® Laundry Soap—then go change your shirt!

Pencil marks? Just take a nice, clean, soft eraser and gently rub the mark away.

If you're one of those confident types who prepares her taxes in pen, treat ink stains by soaking the garment in milk for several hours before laundering. You can also blot with rubbing alcohol or Ink Away®, available at office supply stores.

Paper cut? After disinfecting, secure it with a piece of Scotch® tape. The tape will protect the cut from the air and will also help to ensure that it doesn't get pulled farther apart. And if it doesn't get pulled farther apart, it won't hurt!

If you don't have any tape on hand, even a dab of super glue will help. Really—it's a great little healer. A little dab on the paper cut and no more pain! Is it dangerous? No, just don't use it on deep cuts, and please, don't glue your fingers together. Uncle Sam will not accept that as an excuse for late filing! You did glue your fingers together? A little acetone polish remover will un-stick you—fast!

Okay, you're almost done. You've prepared your return, made out your check, sealed the envelope and are just about to leave the house for the post office when you realize you've forgotten to enclose the check. Dang! Don't despair. Reach for Un-Du™. It will open the envelope right up. No tears, no muss, and you'll be able to re-seal it safely. Un-Du™ is available in home centers, drugstores, hardware stores and discount stores. It has such a wide range of uses. Use it to remove kids' stickers from walls, price stickers from any-thing but fabric and bumper stickers when you change party affiliations. No home should be without it.

If you don't have any Un-Du™, try putting the envelope in the freezer for an hour or so, then roll a pencil under the envelope flaps. With a little bit of care that envelope will open right up faster than you can say "Mata Hari!"

You don't owe? You're my hero! You say you're getting a refund? Give me a call . . .

It's Easter

Now it's time to turn our attention to something more cuddly than the taxman! I have such fond memories of gathering around the table to dye Easter eggs with Dad and the Queen Mother. It's something the King and I love to do, too, and we love to include as many friends and family members as possible. The Queen Mum always insisted on covering the kitchen table with an old plastic tablecloth to prevent those stains from spills (where did you think I got it from?) so that our creations wouldn't harm the table. Here's what else you can do:

Place a clean washcloth or potholder in the bottom of the pan and add cool water. Gently place the eggs in the pan, being careful not to overcrowd them. The cushion on the bottom of the pan will help prevent cracks, but if you add a tablespoon of white vinegar you'll be sure to avoid them altogether. (Vinegar will seal any cracks and help the egg to congeal.) Turn the heat on to medium and bring the eggs to a gentle boil. Continue to boil gently until they are done— about 20 minutes.

Check your eggs for freshness by placing them in a bowl filled with cold water. Eggs that float to the top are old and should be discarded.

• Keep raw eggs fresh in the refrigerator by applying a light coat of solid vegetable shortening. The shortening seals the egg, which keeps the air out and helps the egg last longer.

• If you drop a fresh egg during any of this process, just sprinkle it with a heavy layer of salt, wait several minutes then wipe up with a dry paper towel. The salt will "cook" the egg so that it is easy to remove. A turkey baster also works well.

• Prepare for coloring by putting out several glasses of hot water (plastic will stain). Add 1 tablespoon of vinegar to each cup. The acid in the vinegar will help the dye adhere to the eggs.

• You can use natural things to make great Easter egg dyes. Mustard and turmeric create a wonderful yellow shade, coffee and tea turn eggs tan to brown, red onion skins soaked in water create a purple dye, hot cranberry and cherry juice make vivid reds, and heated orange pop gives you orange! Use your imagination and create additional colors or mixtures.

• Remember: If you plunge hard-boiled eggs into cold water as soon as they are cooked, you won't be bothered with that gray ring on the inside of the egg white.

• Need to know which eggs are boiled and which are raw? Just give them a spin on the counter. A hard-boiled egg will spin easily, whereas a raw egg will wobble.

• One last important piece of information. If you are going to allow your colored Easter eggs to sit out in baskets, don't eat them. Eggs spoil rapidly at room temperature and can cause anyone who eats them to become very sick.

❀❀❀ May ❀❀❀

May is one of my favorite months. The uncertain weather of early spring is a thing of the past, and the whole summer seems to stretch out before us. What better time to get reacquainted with the garden? I came by my love of gardening naturally: I inherited it from my mom! The Queen Mother taught me to garden the natural way, with minimum fuss and *no* chemicals. I'm going to pass that along to you! I'm also going to share some recipes for homemade personal care products because there's nothing nicer than pampering yourself after a warm afternoon in the garden. And because May is the month of Mother's Day, why not treat her, too?

A Garden of Ideas

BEFORE YOU GET STARTED

Get a head start on summer! Plant seeds in an egg carton to which you have added a small amount of soil—don't pack it too hard, and don't let it spill out over the sides. Keep the soil moist, taking care not to overwater. When you've seen the last frost, it's time to pop the seedlings out of the egg container and plant them in the ground. Still impatient? Speed up germination by laying a piece of plastic wrap over the seedlings to keep them moist and warm. Leave the plastic in place until the plants start to poke their heads through the soil.

• Try latex gloves in the garden instead of cloth. They're easier to clean—you can just rinse them under the hose and let them air-dry—and they don't stiffen up like canvas gloves do.

Tie a used fabric softener sheet around your belt to keep mosquitoes away while you garden.

• For a moisturizing treat while gardening, rub your hands with hand cream or petroleum jelly before donning your gloves.

• Don't like to wear gloves? Scraping your fingernails over a bar of soap before you get started will prevent dirt from penetrating under your nails and will protect them from breaking.

• Use a little wagon to haul your supplies around the garden. Check garage sales for good deals.

• Carry a quart spray bottle filled with water and a squirt of liquid dish soap. If you see bugs attacking your flowers, just give them a squirt and they'll vamoose!

• Need a kneeling pad? Take a 2- or 3-inch piece of foam, wrap it in plastic or put it in a large resealaable bag and you're all ready to go.

FERTILIZERS

• Crushed eggshells worked well into the soil make a wonderful fertilizer. Terrific for gardens and houseplants, they aerate the soil, too.

• Bury some used coffee grounds in your garden to provide much-needed acid to soil that has a high alkaline content. You'll notice much greener greens!

• Fish tank water is loaded with nutrients. Use it for gardens and houseplants.

• Plants love starch, so save the water each time you boil noodles or other pasta. Just make sure to let the water cool down first.

• Dampened newspapers placed on the ground around plants will help keep the soil moist and hold weeds at bay. Wet the newspapers well—you need the weight of the water to hold them down—then sprinkle lightly with soil. The papers are biodegradable, so they will eventually dissolve.

PEST CONTROL

• Keep pests such as aphids, mites, and whiteflies off roses, geraniums, hibiscus, and other plants by spraying them with a combination of 1 quart of water and ½ teaspoon of liquid dish soap. Reapply the solution every two weeks.

Planting garlic, parsley or basil among your flowers will deter bugs. Marigolds also work well. Just plant them as an edging around the garden.

• Dissolve 1 to 1½ teaspoons of baking soda in 1 quart of water to kill bugs on flowering plants. Spray every 7 to 10 days.

• Powdered milk can kill aphids on roses. Mix ⅓ cup of powdered milk in one quart of warm water, and spray. The aphids will get stuck in the milk and die. Hose the roses down occasionally and re-apply as needed.

• Here's a great natural way to control black spots on roses. Add 1 tablespoon each of baking soda and vegetable oil to 1 gallon of water. Then add 1 drop of liquid detergent and shake well. Spray directly on the foliage, and spray every 5 to 7 days during humid weather. Make sure to wet both sides of the leaves.

• Chase away pests that feed on your tender plants by mixing 1 tablespoon of hot mustard or red pepper with 1 quart of water. Spray directly on the foliage. One hot taste and the pests will be gone!

WHO KNEW?

• Old panty hose make great ties for plants and tomatoes. They're strong and flexible, but soft enough so that they won't cut into the plant.

Cutting roses and trimming bushes can be a prickly job, but if you grip thorny stems with barbecue tongs or clothespins . . . no more pierced fingers!

• Tuck a bar of soap inside a mesh bag and tie it around the outside faucet. After gardening cleanups will be a breeze.

• Hands that are very dirty can be cleaned with a thick paste of oatmeal and water. Rub well into hands before rinsing and washing as usual.

• Kill weeds with a natural toddy of 1 ounce of white vinegar, 1 ounce of inexpensive gin, and 8 ounces of water. Pour on the weeds and say good-bye.

Keep on the Grass

Morning is the best time to water your lawn. Grass that's damp with dew will absorb water better than grass that's fully dry. Parched grass can be resistant to moisture, so don't wait till your lawn is dehydrated before you bring out the sprinkler. And try not to water your lawn at night if you can avoid it. Night watering can encourage fungus.

You can cut grass that's still damp with morning dew by spraying the blades with vegetable oil. The wet grass won't stick, and you can get on with the rest of the day. Car wax works well too, but it's probably best to skip the drive through the car wash!

How do you know when it's time to water the lawn? I like the barefoot test. If you feel comfortable walking across the grass barefoot—if the lawn isn't crackly and springs back up when you walk across it—there's no need to water. But if the grass feels unpleasantly spiky and lays down flat after you've left the area, it's time to water.

A good soaking of water will promote a healthy lawn. That means strong roots and good color. I put a small empty can of Zack's cat food on the grass when I water the lawn.

When the can is full I know I've given the grass about an inch of water, and that's plenty.

Try not to cut grass too often. A closely manicured lawn may be fine for the golf course, but longer grass is actually healthier because it holds moisture longer. Use the high setting on your mower for best results.

The Cat's Meow

Bothered by moles and gophers? Some people swear by castor bean plants, but the leaves and seedpods are poisonous to children and pets—yikes, that's me! Try human hair instead. Hair is an irritant to these small rodents, but it won't harm them or anything else. Ask your hairdresser for a bag of clippings and stuff the hair into the hole. It won't be long before these little critters move on. (If you have any hair left, you could try knitting a toupee for your uncle Jack.)

If dogs, raccoons or other animals are tipping over your garbage cans, tie a couple of rags soaked in ammonia to the handles. All it takes is one sniff and your garbage can will no longer be attractive to critters. *Dogs . . . sheesh!*

Discourage fleas and flies from gathering around your pet's outside eating and sleeping area by planting rue *(Ruta graveolens)* nearby. You can also rub rue on furniture to keep cats . . . like me, from scratching. Just use care that you don't discolor upholstery.

Keep the neighborhood dogs and cats out of your flowers by mixing equal parts of mothballs and crushed dried red pepper (cayenne) in and around the flower beds. No more four-legged visitors! Not that I would ever do such a thing . . .

Zack

JUST TOOLING AROUND

Take good care of your garden tools and they'll last you a lifetime.

Keep a container of sand in the garage or shed, and push your shovels and trowels into it when you've finished your chores. Sand is a wonderfully natural abrasive. It will clean your tools and stop them from rusting. Not only will this tool-time sandbox prevent dirt from spreading around the garage area, but you'll always know where to find your garden tools!

Spray your garden tools with nonstick cooking spray each time you use them. The dirt will be easy to remove when you are done. In fact, it should fall right off.

Paint the handles of your yard tools a bright color and they will be easier to spot among the green of your yard. Not only that, you'll be able to identify your tools if you loan them out.

If rust has disfigured a metal tool, try rubbing with a stiff wire brush. Scrape a metal file across dull edges and they should come back to life if they're not too dull. Naval jelly sold at hardware stores is also a good alternative for rust on metal. Follow the directions on the container.

You can help protect your tools by applying Clean Shield® Surface Treatment or a thin coat of paste wax to the metal. The wax will form a barrier between the metal and the elements and should retard the growth of rust.

Rough handles mean rough hands, so make sure to take care of your tools. Wood handles that have become jagged and coarse can be made smooth again with a good rubbing of some light-grade sandpaper. Apply a generous coat of linseed oil when you've finished sanding and you'll protect the wood from cracking and splitting.

If you still find the handles too difficult to hold, try wrapping them in tubes of foam insulation, the kind used to insulate water pipes. Slit the foam lengthways, slip it onto the handle, and wrap lightly with heavy-duty tape. Not only will the foam protect your hands from the wood, it will also protect the wood from the elements.

Don't forget to store your tools out of the elements.

A Mom for All Seasons

When you hear the words "Mother's Day" I'm sure you think of your Queen Mother just as I do mine. Naturally, we all want to do something nice for our mothers . . . and naturally is what it's all about. So read on to find out how you can make your own collection of personal care products that are easy to make, and natural too. Give these to your own Queen Mum and every day can be Mother's Day!

LET'S FACE IT

An oatmeal scrub will treat dry skin and draw impurities from your complexion. Mix ¼ cup of oatmeal, 1 teaspoon of honey and enough milk, buttermilk or plain yogurt to make a paste. Apply liberally to your face—making sure to avoid the delicate eye areas—then gently massage in small circular motions. Allow the mask to dry before you rinse with warm water. Once the mask has been removed, give your face an invigorating finish by splashing with cool, clear water. Apply your favorite moisturizer, or for a more thorough facial, follow with the tightening oatmeal mask.

Grandma loved this tightening oatmeal mask, and you will too. Mix 1 tablespoon of oatmeal with the white of 1 egg. Apply to your face and allow to dry. Rinse off using cool water.

Very dry skin? A little mayonnaise added to the tightening oatmeal mask will give you a smooth finish.

Prone to breakouts? Apply a thin mask of milk of magnesia once a week. Allow to dry and rinse with cool water.

Need a four o'clock revival? Try witch hazel. Keep a small bottle in your desk at the office, along with some cotton balls. Dampen the cotton balls with the witch hazel, then blot your face and neck . . . prepare to be revived! It's that easy. Keep the witch hazel in the refrigerator if you can. And for an extra treat, pour some in a spray bottle for an after-workout spritz!

THE EYES HAVE IT

These remedies aren't new, but they're worth repeating.

• A slice of chilled cucumber on each eyelid will relieve tired eyes. And that 15-minute rest won't do you any harm, either!

• Cold tea bags are great for puffy eyes, so keep some on hand in the refrigerator.

• A little bit of Preparation H® helps keep puffy eyes at bay. Just make sure to avoid tear ducts and the eye itself.

• Dab some castor oil on the skin around your eyes before going to bed at night. Stay well away from the eye area, and make sure not to use too much oil.

YOUR CROWNING GLORY

Restore luster to dry hair with a light, natural oil such as corn oil or sunflower oil. Those of you with very dry hair may like to use olive oil, but make sure to use a light touch. Olive oil can be extremely difficult to wash out. Another warning: Oil heats up very quickly and can cause severe burns, so avoid the microwave. The best and safest way to warm oil for a scalp treatment is to place the oil in an egg cup, then put the egg cup inside a mug or small bowl that you have filled with hot or boiling water. Heat the oil to lukewarm—about 1 teaspoon should do—and apply to dry hair with the palm of your hands. Make sure that the shaft and ends are well coated (not saturated, though), but avoid getting oil on your roots, which will weigh hair down. Cover your hair with a plastic bag and try to leave it on as long as you can—overnight is best. Finish with a thorough shampoo, lathering twice. Skip the conditioner and get ready for the compliments!

I hate it when that happens . . .

Static electricity causing your hair to stand on end? Rub your brush and comb with a fabric softener sheet before brushing your hair. No more annoying static!

Mayonnaise also works well—it's a combination of egg *and* oil. Don't heat the mayonnaise or it will separate. Just remove a quantity from the jar—a couple of tablespoons should be fine, unless you have very long hair—and let stand at room temperature for a few hours. Rub on just enough mayonnaise to soak the hair thoroughly (remembering to avoid the roots), and comb through. Leave on for 30 minutes, shampoo well and rinse with water and lemon before that final rinse of cool, clear water.

LET'S SEE A SHOW OF HANDS

Make your own hand cream by mixing 2 parts glycerin to 1 part lemon juice. Massage a little into your hands after washing and at bedtime. This absorbent cream works well and smells lovely!

Soften hardworking hands and feet by rubbing with equal proportions of cooking oil and granulated sugar.

Cuticles may be softened by soaking in a bowl of warm olive oil. Push them gently back with a cotton swab. If cuticles are really dry, coat them with olive oil at bedtime.

Lemon juice is great for removing stains and whitening hands. Bottled or fresh-squeezed, just massage it into hands before washing with good old soap and water.

Your nail polish will last longer if you apply a little white vinegar to each nail. Just coat each nail with a cotton swab prior to applying your nail polish. The acid in the vinegar encourages the polish to stick to the nail so you get better coverage and longer-lasting wear.

Speed up the time it takes to dry nail polish by plunging freshly polished nails into cold water. Shake hands to dry. And to prevent nicks and chipping, brush baby oil on just-polished nails!

Let's Dish!

Of course, nothing says "Mother's Day" like breakfast in bed!

Orange Blossom French Toast

12 slices bread
6 egg yolks
½ cup half-and-half or whole milk
⅓ cup orange juice
1 tablespoon grated orange peel
¼ teaspoon salt
¼ cup butter

Leave bread out to dry overnight.

Next morning, in a medium bowl, slightly beat egg yolks, then mix in half-and-half, orange juice, orange peel, and salt. Dip bread in batter, turning to coat both sides.

Heat butter in skillet and cook bread on both sides until golden.

Serve with syrup and love. Makes 6 servings.

June

Summer—it's finally here. The kids are out of school and it's time to hit the road on the family vacation. Frightened of an endless chorus of *Are we there yet?* It doesn't have to be that way. The kids don't have to be bored and neither do you. There are many things you can do to make that trip a good one—enjoyable *and* safe. So let's put our imaginations to work and have some fun.

Hit the Road, Jack

You're going on a family trip . . . in the car. You may be in there for hours. If that strikes fear in your heart, you're not alone. Hit these pages before hitting the road.

BEFORE YOU LEAVE

It's fun to take a little time away from home. And if you take some time to prep the house before you leave, your homecoming will be that much sweeter.

• Lock the doors and windows, but leave the shades up and curtains open. Put the lights on automatic timer.

• Clean out the refrigerator and remove any perishables.

• Want to know if your freezer has shut off while you've been away? Take a child's ice pop—the ones that come in the clear plastic push-up wrapper—lay it flat to freeze, then prop it against the freezer door. If the freezer goes off while you're away the pop will be hanging over the inside of the door instead of standing straight up. You'll know then that freezer food *isn't* safe to eat.

• Store your valuables in a safe place. The freezer, jewelry box and lingerie drawer are not secure choices.

If you've read about it in a book or newspaper column, chances are it's not a safe place to store your valuables. Burglars read, too. Use your imagination and your discretion.

• Turn off small electrical appliances. Unplug decorative lights and fountains.

• Smokers will want to make sure that ashtrays are empty. Odor from cigarette butts can linger long after the cigarette has been extinguished, and there's nothing worse than coming home to a house that smells like a stale ashtray!

• Suspend delivery of the newspaper and the mail.

• To keep plants watered when you're not at home, gather them up and sit them in the bathtub in about an inch of water. The plants will absorb the water gradually, enough to last a week or two. For those plant pots that don't have a hole in the bottom, fill a glass with water, insert one end of a coarse piece of string in the glass, and bury the other in the plant. Believe it or not, this homemade water wick will keep most plants moist while you're away!

• Leave a key and contact number with a trusted neighbor who will keep an eye on things during your absence.

WHAT TO PACK

No two vacations are alike, so consider what you want from your trip *before* you start to pack. If your weekday routine dictates that you wake at 6:30 to head off for work each morning, then chances are the last thing you want to hear is the ringing of your alarm. If, however, you want to be first in line at Disneyland, you're going to need that clock.

Here's a sample list to get you started:

• Small sewing kit
• Travel hair dryer
• Umbrella or raincoat
• Hunting or fishing license
• Alarm clock
• Swiss army knife
• Small fold-up tote for all those extras you'll buy
• Small amount of laundry detergent for those "oops!"
• Exercise gear
• Camera and film

Take along an almost empty liquid soap container filled with water. It makes a handy cleaner for all those little emergencies.

- Batteries
- A few plastic garbage bags for holding dirty laundry
- Bathing suits
- Plenty of tee shirts
- Tweezers—they come in very handy
- Gallon-size, Ziploc™ bags for damp swimsuits, etc.
- A few clothespins and some safety pins

AND DON'T FORGET THESE NECESSITIES

- Personal medicines and spare eyeglasses
- Children's aspirin and remedies for upset tummies
- Sunglasses, suntan lotion, insect repellant
- A first-aid kit, some paper towels and tissues
- Proof of insurance—auto *and* health
- A duplicate set of car keys
- A spare tire, car jack, flashlight, windshield scraper and emergency repair kit

Spray the front of the car with nonstick cooking spray before you hit the road. Bugs and grime will wash right off.

- A few gallons of fresh water—for you and your radiator
- Maps
- A 1-800 number for credit card companies
- A small notebook and pen
- Picture ID

Backseat Drivers

Traveling with children requires special care and preparation, not to mention a good dose of imagination and patience. So plan ahead. Keep children occupied and try to avoid mishaps *before* they happen. You'll be glad you did.

DOS AND DON'TS FOR A SAFE TRIP

• Do lock all doors and teach your children not to play with the door handles.

• Don't permit children to ride with their heads, arms or hands outside of the car through open windows.

• Do set a good example for your children by buckling up each time you enter the car.

• Don't leave children or pets in the car alone—even for a short time.

• Do make sure that children sit in the backseat.

• Do make sure to make frequent stops so that children can stretch their legs.

• Don't allow children to suck on suckers while riding. A sudden stop could be disastrous.

• Do make sure to take plenty of cold water.

WE'RE NOT FINISHED YET

Children are resilient, but their little bodies can be especially sensitive to the environment. Keep a close eye on small passengers, and be on the lookout for any signs of car sickness and upset tummies. Sometimes a quick stop for some fresh air is all it takes to avoid a problem.

Keep sugared snacks to a minimum. Children high on sugar are not going to be good travelers.

• Keep a new toothbrush in the glove box, along with a small tube of minty toothpaste. If a little one does get carsick and vomit, brushing his teeth afterward will make him feel much better. Just make sure to stay away from sweet or flavored toothpastes, which may aggravate nausea.

• When preparing snack foods for a car journey, make sure to avoid small foods on which a child can choke, like hard candy and peanuts.

• Baby wipes are great for wiping sticky hands and faces—for you *and* your children. They're terrific for cleaning hands after pumping gas at the self-serve, too.

• Little ones will need a change of clothes. Everybody will benefit from having a spare, fresh tee shirt. And don't forget the diapers!

NOW FOR THE FUN STUFF

• Children love to play with office supplies such as Scotch® tape, paper and Post-it® notes—and they can't hurt themselves, either. Don't give children pens or pencils, though, and don't give them scissors.

• Play money is great fun. Your child can set up her own mall in the backseat! Just make sure to avoid giving coins to small children.

• Squares of aluminum foil are great for making sculptures and jewelry, and they can be used again and again. (Don't give foil to young children who may be tempted to put it in their mouths.)

• High-tech kids can still enjoy singing songs and reciting rhymes. Encourage children to make up their own verses. Don't be afraid to get creative!

• Paint books—the kind that already have the paint on the page—are very popular with young children. All you need is a little brush and an inch or so of water in a cup. No fuss and no paint to spill.

• Don't forget the classics. Hangman, tic-tac-toe and "I Spy" are great, as are crossword puzzles.

• Don't forget the bubbles!

• Have your child make some paper bag puppets before you leave. They'll be distracted with their craft, and that will give *you* some uninterrupted time to prepare for the trip. And of course, children will be pleased to take their new creations with them in the car.

• Children love to use binoculars.

• Tattoos, the kind that press on with a wet cloth, are lots of fun.

• Go Fish card games are great. Even children too young to know the game will enjoy playing with the cards. Fifty-two pickup, anyone?

• Everyone knows that books on tape are great for long trips, but small children can get bored just listening. So why not let them record their own book? Many inexpensive cassette players have record buttons, so why not pick up a few tapes at the dollar store and let your child try his on-air talents? He can describe the scenery, make up stories and songs, record a letter to Grandma—he could even interview you!

• Kids love disposable cameras. Consider giving one to each child.

• Toddlers can use licorice laces and Cheerios® or Fruit Loops® to make necklaces and bracelets. When they get bored, they can eat their creations!

🧶 The Cat's Meow

Please make sure that I'm well cared for when you're away. I need food and water of course, but I need some company, too. I get awfully lonely when you're gone. And please make sure to put a note on the door or window that lets people know that I'm inside. Pets can get lost in all the commotion of a fire. I shudder to think of what can happen . . .

If you're taking me with you, please make sure that I have a place of my own in the car, with food and water. Bring my bed if at all possible—just keep me out of the sun.

Give dogs frequent potty breaks and some exercise. Always keep them on a leash, you know how dogs are about running away.

Don't forget my litter tray. A disposable one will be fine. Just don't expect me to go potty at 70 miles per hour with trucks speeding by. I need my privacy.

Make sure that we're wearing our tags, just in case we become lost or disoriented.

🐾 **Zack**

• Buy some small inexpensive toys at the dollar store—things like plastic dinosaurs and little trolls. Wrap them up with brightly colored paper and dole them out as after-snack goodies. Children love unwrapping the toy almost as much as the toy itself. Keep small toys away from little ones who may put them in their mouths.

• Cookie sheets and breakfast-in-bed trays make great portable work spaces for children. Just make sure not to give little ones sharp and potentially dangerous objects such as pens and pencils. The slightest bump can mean disaster when these items are at hand. Crayons and jumbo markers are best.

• Yahtzee® is still a great traveling game.

At the Car Wash

A long trip can take its toll on your car. Here's what to do to get it looking good again—fast!

• Use a paste of baking soda and water to clean the outside windshield so that it shines.

Rust spots can be removed from car bumpers quite easily—just rub with a ball of tinfoil! If the rust is stubborn, try dipping the foil in a glass of cola! (Don't ask . . .)

• Put some baking soda in your car's ashtray. It may not discourage smokers, but it will help neutralize the odor.

• Keep some used fabric softener sheets in your glove box. Use them to wipe the dashboard, clean the air vents, and polish the rearview mirror. Store them in a Ziploc™ bag and you'll still have room for all those maps and fast-food coupons!

• If birds leave you an unwanted gift on the car, simply take some waterless hand cream, working it in well with an old rag. Let sit for several minutes and it should rub right off.

• Remove road tar by saturating it with linseed oil. Apply the oil liberally to the tarred area, let soak for a while and then wipe with an old rag that has been dampened with more linseed oil. Be sure you dispose of the rag outside in the trash.

• Make your own windshield washer fluid by mixing 2 quarts of rubbing alcohol, 1 cup of water, and 1 teaspoon of liquid dish soap. This will not freeze at 30 degrees below. In summer, add 1 pint of rubbing alcohol and 1 teaspoon of liquid dish soap to the car washer container and fill with water. This will keep the windows clean in rain and warm weather.

• Baking soda on a soft, wet cloth is great for cleaning chrome, headlights and enamel.

• Wipe down windshield wiper blades from time to time to remove road film.

• Wash the car in the shade to prevent streaking.

• Use a couple of squirts of liquid dish soap in a bucket of warm water to wash the car. Start at the roof and wash and rinse in sections so that the soap doesn't dry on the car.

• Dry the car with an old bath towel, then for a super shine, rub down with a good-quality chamois.

Father's Day

You don't think we'd let the month go by without celebrating Father's Day, do you? I always think that the best gift is a gift of time. So why not give your father the day off and let him wander the links for a lovely game of golf. And when he comes home, treat his clubs to some tender, loving care . . .

FORE!

Clean golf clubs by lightly rubbing the head and shaft with dry, fine-grade (0000) steel wool. Don't wet the steel wool. Dust with a dry cloth, then use a damp cloth to give the club a final wipe before buffing dry with another clean, soft cloth.

Cleaning the grips is as easy as using soap and water—but the kind of soap you use makes a big difference. Dampen a soft cloth with warm water, then work up a lather with a moisturizing bath bar, such as Dove® or Caress®. Don't use a deodorizing soap, as that will dry out the leather. Rub well to remove the dirt, rinsing the cloth each time it becomes grimy. Repeat until the grip is clean, then reapply the soap and water one last time. Don't rinse—buff with a soft cloth instead. This will keep the grip moist and prevent it from drying out and cracking. For really stubborn dirt or older clubs, work in a little GOJO™ Waterless Hand Cleaner and wipe until clean. Wash with the soap formula and dry well.

Keep the golf glove in a self-closing plastic bag to maintain softness between games. If you need to clean your glove, use the bar soap method prescribed for grips, keeping the glove on your hand to preserve its shape during the process. Work only with a damp cloth, and make sure not to saturate the glove. Finish by buffing with a soft cloth that's clean and dry, and then allow the glove to dry naturally, out of direct light. To restore a dried-out glove, try rubbing a little hand cream into it—while you're wearing it!

Golf shoes need attention, too. Brush the bottoms of the shoes with a firm brush to remove any dirt and debris. If you have been playing on a wet course, don't do this until the shoes are dry. Wash leather shoes as needed with Dove® moisturizing bath soap, removing scuff marks with a little nongel toothpaste or rubbing with a little cuticle remover. For fabric-type shoes, brush well and spot with a damp microfiber cloth. Always keep the shoes treated with a good quality water repellent for those rainy days and dewy mornings. Got a little odor problem? Put some ODORZOUT™ in the toe of an old nylon or sock and keep it in the shoes when you store them to eliminate odor.

Clean golf balls by soaking them in a solution of 1 cup warm water and ¼ cup ammonia. Rub lightly, rinse and lay out to dry. Store extra golf balls in an egg carton. The compartments are the perfect size!

Having trouble identifying your golf and tennis balls? A tiny drop of colored nail polish is just as good as any monogram.

July

Even the most devoted couch potato ventures out of the house in July. So haul out the baseball equipment, hop on that bike, put on the skates, go for a dip in the pool to cure those summertime blues. Sound too energetic for you? Then how about becoming a chaise lounge or hammock potato at a beautiful campsite for a week or so. That can be a wonderfully relaxing way to recharge your body, let the kids run off some steam, and have some quality family time, too.

Let the Games Begin!

Take me out to the ball game . . . just make sure the equipment is clean and in good working order before you do. Otherwise, it's one, two, three strikes you're out!

Wash your baseball glove with a damp cloth and Dove® Moisturizing Bath Bar. Buff with a soft cloth—no rinsing necessary. Keep the leather soft and supple by rubbing with a little petroleum jelly from time to time. Store your ball in the palm of your glove to help keep its shape.

Want to know the best way to clean your bike? Treat it

like a car! Wash the frame with some hot water and a little dishwashing liquid. Rinse well, dry, then apply a coat of car wax to prevent rust. Wash the seat with a little bit of bar soap on a soft cloth and buff dry.

Dented Ping-Pong balls? Just drop them into a bowl of hot water and let them float for a few minutes. Dings should pop right out. Sorry—balls that are cracked or have large dents can't be repaired.

Give your skateboard an occasional wash with good old soap and water. Pay special attention to the wheels by scrubbing with a brush to remove any embedded soil and stones that may slow you down.

Wearing petroleum jelly under your socks can prevent blisters. Apply a thin layer on tender parts before you exercise. And never wear sports socks more than one day running.

Odor can be a problem with skates—both inline and ice. I recommend sprinkling with ODORZOUT™, a first-rate odor eliminator. Shake some into the boot, leave overnight, then gently shake out the following morning. ODORZOUT™ is an odor eliminator, not a perfumed cover-up, so your skates will stay fresher longer. Don't have any? Try baking soda instead.

To clean skate boots, try using a microfiber cloth such as ACT Natural™. The ACT Natural™ cloth can be used on its own—no harmful chemicals to damage those expensive skates.

Before you exchange that hockey equipment for baseball gear, make sure to store your pucks in the freezer. They'll stay harder and more resilient that way!

Who Says There Ain't No Cure?

Summer isn't all fun and games. There are hot nights and insect bites, sunburns to soothe and lawn furniture to clean—what we in the trade commonly refer to as the *summertime blues.* Read on for some handy cures.

• Remove dirt and mildew from a child's wading pool by flushing with warm water and baking soda.

• Sprinkle baby powder on sandy beach bodies and the sand will fall right off.

• A hot night and no a/c? Baby powder on your sheets will absorb moisture and give you a more comfortable night's sleep. What, no baby powder? Use cornstarch instead!

• Wipe exposed skin with undiluted white vinegar to discourage biting insects.

• Apply a compress of warm salt water if you're bitten by a mosquito or chigger. For long-lasting itch relief, mix a little salt and solid shortening, such as Crisco®, and dab it directly on the bite.

That frosty film on the carton of ice cream is not a protective coating, and it can be prevented. Just cover the top of the ice cream with wax paper and press firmly. No more "protective crystals"!

• Deodorant that contains aluminum (and most do) can be put on a bite to control the itch.

• Sliding doors get a lot of use in the summer, so be sure to keep tracks clean and well lubricated. The easiest way? Spritz tracks with furniture polish, then wipe with a dry cloth or paper towel. The polish will pick up grime, and will keep the tracks better lubricated than a cleanser would. If you want to add some glide between cleanings, just wipe the tracks with a square of waxed paper. Works every time!

• A plastic shower liner makes a great tablecloth. It's washable and inexpensive.

• Sheets make better beach blankets than blankets. They don't hold sand and they're easier to launder when you get home. Pick up some spares at a thrift store.

• Black pepper will deter ants. Just sprinkle under rugs or cupboard liners. Silverfish can be kept at bay with Epsom salts: Just shake some in cupboards and under lining paper in drawers.

• Put sunburned kids in a cool (not cold) baking soda bath for half an hour. This also works well for chickenpox and mosquito bites.

I hate it when that happens . . .

Tar on bare feet? Remove it by rubbing vigorously with toothpaste.

• No need to use chemicals or expensive products to clean lawn furniture. Just rinse with warm water and baking soda.

Sprinkle dry baking soda directly on stubborn marks—this natural abrasive will take them right off!

Camping

If slow room service is your idea of camping, you may want to skip this section.

THE NECESSITIES

• Campsites can be very dark in the evening, so make sure to bring along a torch, a candle or flashlight. Even better, bring along all three. And don't forget the batteries!

• Remember that Swiss army knife you got for Christmas three years ago? Now's the time to use it. You'll need some good kitchen knives, too, so don't forget to bring those as well.

• Toilet paper in a lidded coffee can to keep it dry. Need I say more?

• Bring a few candles, a votive or tea light.

• Make sure to bring along a little dishwashing liquid, a scouring pad and some absorbent towels.

• A cooked breakfast is one of the joys of camping, but bacon and eggs are *not* finger foods. Don't forget the cutlery, cooking utensils, a pot to boil water in, and a frying pan.

Rubbing two sticks together to make a fire is highly overrated. Don't try to be macho. Bring along matches or a lighter.

• Bring along a length of nylon rope. You can use it for dozens of things, such as drying clothes, elevating food so that animals don't get at it, and knocking up emergency shelter. You can even use it to replace those lost guy ropes. Use your imagination . . . just don't tie up the kids!

• Bandannas are wonderfully versatile. They make good napkins, facecloths, bandages and slings. Tuck one under the back of your baseball cap to keep the sun off your neck, foreign-legion style!

• A first-aid kit is a must. Make sure yours is stocked with bandages, antiseptic, tweezers, a thin needle for splinters, Imodium® for those tummy troubles, aspirin or aspirin-substitute, sunscreen and sunburn relief, insect repellent and a whistle to call for help in an emergency.

Cell phones are great, but the batteries on whistles never run down.

• Bring soap. You can find the water when you get there.

• Dental floss and a darning needle will come in handy for quick repairs to holes in clothes and tents.

• Duct tape is indispensable.

FIRE STARTERS

There's an easy way to dry out wet kindling. Construct a small tepee out of your kindling, making sure to leave an opening into which you can insert a tea light or votive candle. Insert the lighted candle, then watch as the kindling crackles and dries. You should have a fire under way by the time the candle has burned down.

Pinecones make great kindling. They heat up fast and burn for a long time.

Bring along a few cardboard tubes from paper towels or toilet paper. Twist a few sheets of newspaper to fit inside the tube (I find the business section works best), making sure to leave some paper hanging out the ends. Toss a few of these in with twigs and wood and you'll have a roaring fire in no time!

My dad and I learned—quite accidentally—that grease from cooking pans makes a great fire starter! Use paper towels to wipe up the grease from pots and pans, then store them in self-closing plastic bags. The next time you need to start a campfire, wrap some twigs in the paper and set them alight!

Keeping matches dry can be a challenge, but if you dip the match head and part of the matchstick into some candle wax, it will resist water. Light as usual—the act of striking the match will remove the wax. (This only works on wooden matches, not cardboard.)

Rub the outside of pots and pans with a bar of soap before you use them. Do this to both the bottom and sides of the pan, and soot will wipe right off, along with the soap.

LOITERING WITHIN YOUR TENT

• Rocks, twigs and other sharp objects may damage your tent, so make sure the ground is clear before you set up camp.

- Avoid wearing heavy shoes inside the tent.

- Use extreme caution around open flames. Nylon tents melt easily.

- Pack tent poles carefully to avoid punctures.

- Prolonged exposure to direct sunlight can weaken tent fibers, so wherever possible, set up the tent in a shaded area.

- A strip of glow-in-the-dark tape wrapped around tent stakes will ensure that you never trip over them again!

- Drive tent stakes twelve inches into the ground to provide adequate stability, even in the wind. The stakes should be at a 45-degree angle, slanting *away* from the tent. Paint each stake at the 12-inch mark and you'll never have to guess again!

CLEANING YOUR TENT

Make sure to store your tent correctly—that means cleaning it first. With proper care your tent can last for years.

Shake off all loose debris before packing and storing the tent. Clean any spots with a wet brush rubbed over a bar of Fels-Naptha Soap®, then rinse. Air-dry thoroughly. A damp tent is a breeding ground for mildew.

Stakes should be stored alongside the tent, but make sure to put them in a canvas bag or even a few old pillowcases—something to ensure that the stakes will not tear or puncture the tent itself.

Take action at the first sign of mildew—an organic rotting odor, black spots or a powdery white smudge. Sponge the tent with a solution of ½ cup of Lysol® and 1 gallon of warm water. Allow to dry on the tent (think *leave-in conditioner*) and air-dry thoroughly prior to storing. For advanced mildew use a combination of 1 cup of lemon juice (real or bottled) and 1 gallon of warm water. Rub onto visible mildew and allow to dry facing the sun.

Spray zippers with a silicone lubricant to ensure smooth action and prevent freezing. Rubbing with paraffin or candle wax works well, too.

REPAIRING YOUR TENT

Stakes and tent poles cause the majority of tears in canvas tents. Either the pole slips and tears the fabric next to the eyelet, or the canvas itself is tied too tightly to the ground stakes. Bear this in mind when setting up your tent.

Canvas is too heavy for most home sewing machines, so if your tent is generally in good condition, you may want to consider getting it repaired by a tent or sail maker.

For a cheaper alternative, glue an appropriate-sized square of canvas to the tent. Make sure you overlap the tear by about one to two inches. Putting a patch on both sides of the tent will reinforce the repair. Use fabric glue or even a hot glue gun and remember to waterproof the repair once the glue is dry.

Duct tape is great for making emergency repairs. Just make sure to tape both sides of the tear. And remember: This is just an interim measure. Have your tent properly repaired once you get back home.

Nylon or cotton hiking-type tents can be repaired on a home sewing machine. Look for patch kits, available where tents are sold.

Never underestimate the power of a large darning needle and dental floss.

IT'S IN THE BAG

Keep your sleeping bag clean and mildew free by washing it in a large capacity machine. Add ½ cup of 20 Mule Team® Borax to the water along with your detergent, and ½ cup of white vinegar in the rinse instead of fabric softener.

Make sure that the sleeping bag is totally dry before storing to prevent mildew. When ready to store, place about a quarter cup of ODORZOUT™ in a nylon stocking and tuck inside the sleeping bag to prevent odors. A good sprinkling of baking soda will help to keep it fresh, too. Store your sleeping bag inside a king-size pillowcase to keep it clean.

August

Where did the summer go? Seems like only yesterday we were preparing the garden for spring, and now we're thinking about how to make the most of this final summer month. I hate to be a drag, but it's time to give your house the once-over before autumn starts. That means paying attention to those tasks that everybody seems to ignore—cleaning the driveway *and* the gutters. It's not all chores, though. We still have some time for that last summer picnic!

Driveway Dilemmas

Driveways take quite a beating, but we never seem to pay much attention to them—until they're covered with oil spills and weeds. Put off caring for your driveway, and like most jobs, it will become more difficult and time-consuming when you finally do get around to it. So sweep your driveway regularly—say, once a month in the summer—and wash it thoroughly once a year. You'll be glad you did.

Give your driveway a good sweep. Use a stiff push broom or long-handle brush, and make short brisk strokes to direct debris away from the center of the driveway.

• Wash concrete driveways with a simple solution of water and washing soda. Dissolve 1 cup of Arm and Hammer Washing Soda™ in a bucket of warm water and apply to the driveway with a long-handle brush or stiff push broom. Scrub well, then rinse with clear water.

• Oven cleaner works well for those really tough stains. Spray it on, let sit for a few hours, and then rinse well. Just make sure to keep the kids and pets a good distance away.

• For old marks and blotches, apply a heavy layer of a good laundry stain remover, such as Zout®, and allow it to sit for five minutes before sprinkling with powdered laundry detergent. Apply a small amount of water to get a good lather going, then scrub with a stiff broom and rinse well.

• Kitty Litter™ is good at absorbing oil. Just make sure to grind it into the stain with your feet.

• Patio blocks can be cleaned with washing soda or laundry stain remover. Don't use the oven cleaner method, though. It can remove color and damage the blocks.

• Kill weeds that grow through the cracks in driveways and patios by saturating them with 1 gallon of warm water to which you have added ¼ cup of salt.

• Prevent weeds from growing in these cracks by sprinkling salt directly into the crevices. That's all there is to it—just let nature do the rest.

Get Your Mind *into* the Gutter!

Gutters are designed to carry rainwater and melting snow off your roof and away from your house. They are not storage places for leaves, Frisbees™, and tennis balls. Keep them clean.

Check your gutters to see if they're in good working order by spraying a hose directly into the trough. If the water runs through the trough and out the spout, you're in good shape. If, however, the water flows over the sides, it's time to give those gutters a good cleaning.

Use a ladder to clean gutters. Never approach them from the roof. That's asking for trouble. If the ground beneath your ladder is soft, sit the legs of the ladder into a couple of small cans, such as those from tuna fish. The cans will help distribute the weight, and the ladder won't slope or sink into the ground at uneven levels.

Once you're confident that the ladder is secure, climb to the height of the gutters and, wearing rubber gloves, scoop out the debris that's collected there. Hang a couple of shopping bags onto your ladder and use them to hold the debris. When one is full, just toss it to the ground and start filling the next. (Just don't forget to shout, "Look out below!")

Once you've removed the debris, flush the spout with water to make sure it flows freely. Usually, a forceful stream of water directed down the spout will be strong enough to push out anything that's blocking it. If that doesn't work, try inserting the hose *up* the spout. That should loosen the debris. One final blast of water from the top down should then be enough to dislodge whatever is blocking it.

You can avoid a lot of this hassle next year by placing a screen or netting over the gutters, which will prevent leaves and other debris from settling.

Time for a Picnic

A sunny day, a brightly colored checkered tablecloth, something good to eat . . . sounds like heaven to me! There's nothing quite like a picnic to round off an afternoon of outdoor fun, but insects and food poisoning can ruin the day. Read on to find out how to ward off those uninvited guests, as well as for advice on how to relieve that burn from the last of the summer sun. Oh, and let's not forget how to care for and clean that barbecue grill!

DON'T BUG ME

• Insects are attracted to intense colors—bright *and* dark. Bear this in mind when selecting tablecloths and paper plates, as well as your clothes for the day. This is not the time to be bold!

• Citronella candles are great standbys. No picnic should be without them.

• Insects love grapes, melon, and sweet fruit drinks, as well as strongly scented foods, such as tuna, strong cheeses, and meats. Think about this as you prepare your picnic.

• Choose a picnic site that's away from rivers, lakes, and streams. Insects tend to gather around water.

Flies ruining your picnic? Keep them away by wiping the table with some undiluted white vinegar or laying some citrus peels on the tablecloth.

- Odors can broadcast mealtimes to insects, so keep foods sealed in plastic containers until you're ready to eat.

- Make sure to cover serving plates so insects can't touch down on your meal—even for a moment. Domed food covers are great, as are pieces of inexpensive nylon netting. Don't have either? Try turning a large bowl upside down over platters.

- Don't let a bug surprise you in your soda or juice. Cover the glass with a piece of aluminum foil and then push a straw through it.

- Ants can't make it through water, so the best way to deter them is by sitting the legs of your picnic table in tin cans filled with water. Disposable pie tins or old Frisbees™ work well for tables with thicker legs.

- Entice insects away from your picnic by giving them a picnic of their own. Put a pie plate filled with water and sugar several yards away from your eating area. The bugs will rush to their meal, leaving you alone to enjoy yours! (Don't forget to pick up the pie plate before you leave.)

Cuts and scrapes may come with outdoor fun, but the ouch that comes with bandage removal doesn't have to. Just rub some baby oil around the bandage before pulling it off.

FOOD FOR THOUGHT

Picnics may be the ultimate in casual eating, but that doesn't mean you should be casual about the way you prepare and store the food. Bacteria thrive in hot weather; that's why it's

easy to become sick from food poisoning. So take a few precautions and have a lovely, stress-free day.

• Keep hot foods hot and cold foods cold. That means
making sure you have one cooler set aside for cold foods,
and one for hot.

*A tear or hole in a picnic cooler
can be repaired with candle wax. Gently warm the
bottom of a candle over a flame, then rub it on the tear until
the seam can no longer be noticed. A wax scar will form,
and that should prevent further splitting.*

• Insulate foods by wrapping them in layers of newspaper or brown paper grocery bags.

• Large blocks of ice keep food colder and last longer
than their smaller counterparts, so use your imagination
when choosing containers for ice. Milk cartons, for example, do a great job! Rinse out the carton (no need to use
soap), fill it with water about two inches from the top, then
pop it into the freezer until you're ready to go. Don't cut
the top off, and don't tear it open, either. Resealing the
spout once you're ready to go will ensure that this ice block
stays cold a long time.

• Think of that foam cooler as your "hot chest." Put all
of your hot foods together, wrap them well in layers of
paper, and the combined heat will create a thermos to keep
everything hot for a few hours.

• Add mayonnaise to foods when you're ready to eat

them, not before. It's not the mayonnaise that's the problem; it's usually the foods you mix with it that carry bacteria. Mayonnaise deteriorates quickly in warm conditions, and can act as a host for bacteria-growing food.

I hate it when that happens . . .
Ketchup too slow for your liking? Tap firmly on the side of the bottle, and the ketchup will come right out.

• Ketchup and mustard deteriorate in hot weather, so leave the big bottles at home. Now's the time to use up all those extra packets of ketchup and mustard you picked up at fast-food restaurants.

• Don't eat picnic leftovers or food left out for more than two hours.

• If it smells or looks bad, throw it out. Don't take chances.

THE GRILL DRILL

Never use gasoline or kerosene to start a fire. These substances are extremely flammable and very difficult to control—and they're not safe to use around food, either.

Don't try to revive a smoldering fire with a squirt of charcoal lighter fluid. The fire could flare up and you could be engulfed in flames. Revive a fire by dampening a few fresh pieces of charcoal with lighter fluid and carefully placing them—one at a time—in with the old coals.

Dispose of ashes with care. Douse them with water, stirring them with a metal fork, then douse with yet more water. You can also dispose of ashes by dumping them into a metal can. Wait at least 24 hours before putting in with other garbage.

Clean the exterior of gas and charcoal grills with GOJO Crème Waterless Hand Cleaner™. Dip a paper towel into the GOJO™, work it into the outside of the grill, and watch the dirt, grease and barbecue sauce come right off! Buff with a clean paper towel and the grill will sparkle like new—with the added benefit of a nice protective coating.

The easiest way to clean a grill rack? Lay the cool rack upside down on the grass and leave it overnight. The dew will work to soften any burned-on food and the next morning you can simply wipe it off!

Grilling at the beach? Clean the grill rack by rubbing it with sand!

Place a layer of sand in the bottom of a charcoal grill to prevent the charcoal from burning through the bottom.

Remove burned-on foods with black coffee. Just pour the coffee over a hot grill rack and wipe with aluminum foil.

The Hot News on Sunburn

Ouch! You forgot the sunscreen and now the damage has been done. It happens to the best of us. Sunburns hurt. Bad.

But there are some steps you can take to cool the heat and soothe the pain. Read on.

• A cool bath helps. Shake in some baking soda, or about ½ cup of salt. Soak for about 30 minutes or so, then apply aloe gel to still-damp skin to keep the temperature down. (Works on mosquito bites and chickenpox, too!)

• A thin layer of Preparation H® is soothing to hot, itchy skin and is especially good on delicate facial areas. Yes, I am serious.

• Make up compresses of 1 part milk to 3 parts water, then lay on burned areas for soothing relief. The protein in the milk will draw out the heat.

• Moist tea bags can offer much-needed relief to eyelids that are burned and swollen. Lay the cold bags over closed eyes, then relax for 30 minutes or so.

• Heavy lotions can trap heat rather than soothe it, so try gels instead, particularly those containing aloe.

• Your grandmother may remember this old-fashioned remedy: Whip 1 egg white with 1 teaspoon of castor oil, then apply to affected areas. Let dry. Rinse off with cool water.

• Spraying on a 50/50 solution of cider vinegar and tepid water will cool the burn on contact.

• Vitamin E is a wonderful moisturizer for burned skin.

The Cat's Meow

Don't you hate it when pet food gets dry and sticks to the bowl? I know I do—and I'm not the one who has to clean it out! There is a solution, though: Give the bowl a quick spritz of nonstick cooking spray before dishing out the food. No more stuck-on food. No more difficult cleaning jobs.

A little bit of oil in my food will also help with that bowl cleanup. And it's also good for my coat!

A lot of people like to use Dustbusters® to clean up scatterings of cat litter (apparently not all kitties are as fastidious as I am), but not many of them know that a used dryer fabric sheet makes a great addition to the filter. Easy to clean and fresh smelling, too!

Zack

September

Children are grumbling. Parents are rejoicing. It must be September—back to school! Doesn't matter if you're dealing with a first grader or a high school senior (or whether you yourself are heading back to college), going back to school can be exhilarating—and stressful. So get organized. Plan ahead. Establish rules. Consider your schedule and your family's needs, and with a little bit of imagination, you can get the school year off to a good start.

School Daze

FIRST THINGS FIRST

Try not to buy any new clothes for your kids without taking stock of what you have on hand. Go through their closets first, *then* hit the back-to-school sales.

Take an afternoon—a rainy one if you can—and sift through your children's closets. If they're at an age when they're interested in what they wear, enlist their help and consider it a joint project. This is a terrific opportunity to show them the benefits of being organized. Come armed with a few large plastic bags and some silly jokes. Let them pick the music to play and let them decide (with your help) what stays and what goes. The more you involve your children in the process, the more likely they are to cooperate. And if there are any squabbles down the road; well, remind them that the choices were made by both of you!

The first step to an organized closet? Get rid of anything that's too small or that you know won't be worn anymore. If repairs are needed, now's the time to do them. Hem hems, fix zips, sew on buttons and tend to any mending that you can. Then make use of those large plastic bags and get rid of whatever can't be used. Can't find a mate to that sock? Get rid of it. Elastic gone on those underpants? Use them as cleaning rags. Be ruthless. If an item of clothing is not up to the task, throw it out. Those torn jeans may be old favorites, but if they're ripped beyond repair, let your son say farewell to them and put them in the trash. That pink blouse may have been your daughter's favorite, but if it didn't fit her last year, it's not going to fit her now. Donate the blouse to a thrift shop and move on to the next item. This is no time to be sentimental. You've got a closet to organize.

Now look into that pared-down closet and see what you've got left. At this point, I like to remove everything so I can organize it anew. Take all the clothes out of the closet and put them on the bed. You might find it easier to make separate piles—one for shirts or blouses, one for pants, one for skirts, sweaters, and so on. Your child's style will dictate how many different mounds of clothes you have. You don't have to be precise with your categories, just separate clothes into logical groups so they're easier to put back.

Now comes the fun part. There's only one rule when it

comes to organizing: It has to work for you, and you have to be consistent. (Well, I guess that's two, but who's counting?) So, if your daughter wants to organize her closet by colors, let her. If your son wants to organize his clothes by day of the week, let him. Just make sure your child knows that he or she will be responsible for the upkeep of the system, *every single day.* Take the time to talk to your child. Offer her some choices. Blouses here, tee shirts there, skirts over here and pants down there. If your daughter rarely wears those two blue dresses and is keeping them for special occasions, you may want to suggest that she keep them near the back of her closet and bring more frequently worn items to the front. If your son wears mostly tees and sweatshirts, ask him if he'd rather keep these items in baskets. (Do you know a child who *likes* to hang up his clothes?) Talk about the best ways of organizing and you may come up with some nifty ideas that will suit your child well. Be imaginative and flexible. The more realistic you are in planning the closet, the more likely your child is to keep it tidy. And isn't that what it's all about?

A few suggestions:

• Make it easy for your child to put his clothes away by installing hooks at easy-to-reach levels.

• Install low bars so that little ones can hang up their own clothes.

• Baskets and buckets are great for holding children's socks and underwear.

• Let your child select some bright hangers in her favorite colors. Clothes are less likely to end up on the floor that way.

• A baseball-cap holder is great for that Little-League enthusiast.

• Everyone knows that an over-the-door shoe rack is great for shoes. It's also great for tee shirts, gym clothes, swimsuits and dance gear.

• Use plastic storage bins to hold clothes that aren't used daily. And make sure to label them well. If your child is too young to read, let him draw pictures so he knows what's inside.

• Encourage children to make use of all of the racks and shelves in their closets—the ones they can reach, anyway.

• Give each child a colorful laundry hamper, and let older children know that they're responsible for bringing their laundry down to the laundry room.

One last thing: Now that your children know the work that goes into organizing a closet, you might want to remind them of that old adage *Work saved is work done.* Encourage your children to keep their closets organized and their clothes clean. Remind them to put away their school clothes when they remove them, not several hours later when the wrinkles have had time to set. Who knows . . . they might even listen!

CLOTHES CALLS

• When hitting those back-to-school sales, remember to save some money for those new fads that show up the first few weeks of school—those things the kids *just can't* do without.

• Read the care labels on new clothes. Make sure you know whether an item has to be handwashed or dry-cleaned *before* you buy it.

• If your child is having problems with a zipper, try rubbing a pencil over it a few times. The graphite will help the zipper to glide as smooth as ice!

New school shoes causing your child to slip?
Score the soles with the tines of a fork.

• If new school clothes are too stiff—a problem with jeans especially—break them in by throwing ½ a cup of table salt in with the wash. They'll come out nice and soft!

JUST FIVE MORE MINUTES

I wish I could give you more time in the morning, but I'm a Queen, not a magician. There are, however, some things you can do to make your mornings less hectic.

The school bus leaves in ten minutes and all across the country kids are screaming, "I can't find it!" Don't let this happen to you. Help each child select a designated spot for books, homework and sports equipment—plus anything else they need to take to school in the morning. Baskets are great, as are bright plastic buckets. Canvas bags hanging on coatracks are good, too.

Designate another safe place for report cards (did I just shiver?), notes from teachers, and permission slips that need to be signed. And let your children know, firmly, that the morning of is *not* the time for signatures.

An over-the-door shoe rack in see-through plastic can be great for holding those small items that kids never seem to be without—and never seem willing to leave the house without. Label a few pockets for each child and tell them it's their own little holding bay. These pouches can be used to hold skipping ropes, GameBoys™, caps and small toys, not to mention hats, scarves and mittens. Give top pockets to older kids and save the easy-to-reach pouches at the bottom for the little ones.

Television is a great distraction. Keep the TV off in the morning and you'll all save time.

If kids want to agonize over what goes with what (not to mention who's *wearing* what), that's fine. Just remind them that 8:00 in the morning is not the time to be doing it. Save yourself a headache and let the kids select what they want to wear to school, but get them into the habit of setting out their clothes *the night before.*

WHO'S ON FIRST?

A large family calendar is a must. Keep it displayed in a location that's prominent *and* convenient. Older children can be taught to log in their own events; just make sure they tell you first. Use the calendar for school functions, sports events, doctor's appointments and birthday parties. Keep a bulletin board nearby. You can use that to hold any relevant papers, like invitations, cards and notes.

A daily visit to your family calendar is not a bad idea. It just takes a minute or so to prevent overlaps that may lead to conflicts.

Get your children in the habit of looking at the calendar, too. Show them how their week is shaping up *before* they enter into it. Let your children know that four busy days in a row might not be such a good idea, and encourage them to use their calendar to make choices. Everybody needs to be reminded that they don't have to say *yes* to everything.

If nothing's scheduled on a particular day, why not use the calendar for other things? Jot down a knock-knock joke or an encouraging word about a child's performance. An organized life doesn't have to be boring!

Accept the fact that things don't always run smoothly. Some days *are* better than others. Take a deep breath and don't sweat it. Tomorrow offers another chance to get it right.

GET IT OFF YOUR CHEST

Now that you're in the mood to get organized, why not extend the project for just a few more minutes and tidy up your medicine chest? This small but important project could mean a lot to your family's safety.

Remove everything from the cabinet and place the contents onto a large flat surface, such as a table. Again, organize the contents into logical groups. Medicines here, bandages there, and so on. Now:

- Toss out anything that doesn't have a label.

- Get rid of any medicines that have passed their expiration dates.

- Take note of any duplicates you may have but don't, for heaven's sake, combine them. You may have two half-empty bottles of aspirin, but putting them together in the same bottle to save space is a bad idea, especially if they have different expiration dates.

- Blister-pack pills are often separated from their boxes. If you aren't certain of the medication or if you don't know the date of expiration, get rid of them. This is no time to be frugal.

- Chances are, you have at least one tensor bandage that's lost its elasticity. Get rid of it.

Cleaning out a medicine chest is similar to cleaning out a closet, except you don't have to sew on any buttons!

Unwanted medications can still be dangerous, so make sure to dispose of them safely. Flushing them down the toilet may be satisfying in a dramatic sort of way, but that can be bad for the environment. Don't just toss pills in the garbage, either. They can be deadly to children and animals. The best way to get rid of medication is to put it in a child-proof container, then in another jar (which you seal), and then safely in the garbage. Don't take chances.

Despite its name, the medicine chest is probably the worst place to store medicines. Not only does it suffer fluctuations in temperature, but it's damp and steamy, too!

Take this time to clean out the shelves of your medicine chest. Metal shelves can be cleaned with a little bit of baking soda and water. Glass shelves can be cleaned with vinegar. Make sure that surfaces are dry before restocking, and take this opportunity to be a rebel and store anything *but* your medicines in your medicine chest. That's right!

Store your medication in a place that is clean, dry and safe from curious youngsters. Save the medicine chest for the cotton balls.

The Last Word, and a Very Important One at That!

Carbon monoxide is a tasteless, odorless killer. It can be released by wood-burning stoves, fireplaces, furnaces, kerosene lamps and gas-fired heaters, and it occurs when these items burn without enough oxygen. When fresh air is restricted, carbon monoxide can build up in your home and cause an irregular heartbeat, headaches and fatigue. In very high amounts, it can cause death.

Please, take the following precautions against this silent killer:

• Ensure that adequate air is available in any room that contains a gas-burning appliance.

• Have your furnace, chimneys and flues checked regularly for cracks and leaks.

• Make certain that door and stovepipe connections fit tightly on all old wood-burning stoves.

• Use a range hood and fan with a gas stove.

• Keep a window slightly open when using a space heater that operates on oil, gas or kerosene.

• Never barbecue in a house or closed garage.

• Always make sure the garage door is open when running the car.

The most important thing to do to protect yourself and your family is to purchase a carbon monoxide detector. It's not expensive, but it may turn out to be priceless.

October

The days are getting shorter. The nights are getting longer. And that nip in the air tells us without a doubt that the seasons are changing. I hate to be the one to mention this, but it's time to get ready for the colder months. So, let's store our summer clothes and soon-to-be out-of-season sports and gardening equipment. Then let's move inside and turn our thoughts to brighter things, like lighting fixtures. Once we've done that, we can get dressed up in costumes and scare the living daylights out of the neighbors. What else is Halloween for?

Storing Summer Clothes

Summer is finally over and now it's time to store your warm weather clothes. Try to avoid the temptation to just push them to one side of your closet. You'll feel better organized all year long if you make the effort to adjust your closet to the seasons. You won't have so many items to sift through when looking for something to wear, and your clothes are less likely to become wrinkled in the crush.

Clothes should be washed before storage; otherwise, stains will have a nice long time to set, and you'll never get them out. It's best to have everything laundered (or dry-cleaned, as the case may be), even if they seem to be clean. Some stains are hard to detect and only materialize over time, like a rash. Best to tackle them right away.

Another good reason to launder clothes before storing them? Moths are attracted to your scent.

Try to avoid using fabric softener on clothes you're about to store. Fabric softener can leave grease spots, which can attract undesirables and weaken fibers. Best to forego the softener, or use a vinegar rinse

For surprise spots on washable clothes, try using ½ cup of hydrogen peroxide and 1 teaspoon of ammonia. Saturate the stain and allow to sit for 30 minutes. Then launder. Zout® Stain Remover is also great on old stains; use as directed.

Make sure that swimsuits are washed before storing them. Chlorine residue can damage fibers and may give you a nasty shock when you head to the beach next year. It's best to wash swimsuits using your machine's gentle cycle and cold water along with your favorite laundry detergent. (If you have been swimming in salt water, soak the suit in cold water for 15 minutes *before* washing.) If you handwash your suit, make sure to rinse well to get rid of all detergent. Air-dry your suit out of the sun. Don't put it in the dryer. Heat can break down the elastic and spandex that keeps the shape of your swimsuit.

Don't forget to protect your natural fibers from those natural predators: moths. Mothballs work well, although some people find the odor offensive. Cedar chips are also reliable. Just insert a handful into the container with your clothes. Perhaps the best deterrent, though, is this lovely homemade citrus remedy: Take some oranges, grapefruit, lemons or limes, remove the peels and cut them into thin strips. Place the strips on a cookie sheet (making sure it's clean) and leave in a warm place to dry. You can also speed the drying process by placing the tray in a 300-degree oven. Preheat the oven, then turn it off before putting in your citrus tray. Prolonged heat will burn the peels. Once the peels are dry and cool, put them into clothes pockets, storage drawers or boxes. No nasty smells, and no damage from moths, either.

Suitcases come in handy for storing seasonal clothes, but I like under-the-bed storage boxes best. Choose between cardboard or plastic, whichever suits your space and budget. I like the transparent plastic boxes because they allow me to see at a glance what's inside. Nevertheless, I also tape a list of the contents to the top of the box so I can get to things in a hurry, if need be. (I *am* an organized Queen!)

Don't store clothes in plastic dry cleaner bags.
They can cause yellowing.

Be creative as to *where* you store your boxes. Under-the-bed storage boxes don't have to go under the bed. Look at the unused space in children's closets, for example. And who says that the linen closet it strictly for linens? Just be careful of storing clothes in the basement, attic, or other places where mold and mildew can damage clothes.

Give some thought as to how you want to pack the boxes *before* you start the process. Use separate storage receptacles for each person, try not to overstuff boxes, and be sure to group types of clothes together. You'll be glad you did when, next summer, you find how easy it is to unpack boxes that have already been organized with care.

Bring the Outdoors In

Now that summer is drawing to a close, it's time to take a few steps to make sure that your tools and summer gear are safe and dry for the winter ahead. A word of caution: If you store your seasonal equipment in the garage (and most of us do), don't forget to leave room for your car!

• Lawn chairs and summer gear can be suspended from the ceiling of your garage with sturdy hooks.

• Open rafters make great storage space, too. Secure items there with bungee cords.

• Don't overlook the simple solutions. A shopping bag hung on a nail can be great for storing small and medium-sized balls.

• An inexpensive string hammock, the type you might use to display a child's collection of stuffed animals, makes a great home for soccer balls and other large items.

• Pegboards are endlessly versatile. Use them to hold hand tools and other small equipment. There's a reason they've stood the test of time!

• Sand doesn't freeze, so store your small gardening tools in the same container of sand that you've been using all summer.

• Garden hoses can crack and split in severely cold weather, so store them inside. Just make sure they're empty first. Pockets of water can collect and freeze in cold weather, and that can result in a tear.

• Take steps to ensure that your lawn mower will start in the spring. Old, unleaded fuel can solidify over winter and that will clog up the workings on your mower. Empty the gas tank and then run the mower till it stops. Only then should you store it for the winter.

Let There Be Light

Now that it's too cold for outdoor lanterns and citronella candles, let's turn our attention to indoor lighting, namely, the main light in your dining area. It may not be the chandelier from *The Phantom of the Opera,* but the light over your dining room table is still important. Keep it clean and sparkling—it will reflect well on you.

Use a premoistened alcohol wipe to quickly shine chandelier crystals for no drips and lots of sparkle!

Chandeliers have a reputation of being difficult to clean, but it doesn't have to be that way. First, turn off the light and give the bulbs a chance to cool down—don't start until they're cool to the touch. Place a small, plastic snack bag over each bulb and secure with a twist tie to prevent moisture from seeping into the socket. Next, position a table directly under the chandelier, covering it with a sturdy plastic table cover and a good layer of old rags (towels work well). This will give you a work base and will also catch the cleaning solution as it drips off the chandelier.

Now for the cleaning solution: Make a mixture of 2 cups of warm water, ½ cup of rubbing alcohol and 2 tablespoons of an automatic dishwasher spot stopper, such as Jet Dry™. Pour the solution into a spray bottle—you can pick them up quite cheaply at the dollar store—then spray the chandelier liberally. Allow it to drip-dry. Pour the leftover solution in a cup and you can use it to hand-dip the crystal teardrops or other decorative hanging pieces. No need to remove them from the chandelier; just dip them and let them drip-dry. The chandelier will be sparkling.

I hate it when that happens . . .

If a lightbulb breaks off in the socket, just grab a bar of soap and push it into the jagged edges. Turn the soap counterclockwise and presto! You've safely removed the broken bulb!

But wait: You're not finished—not until you clean the bulbs themselves. Lightbulbs collect dust and that prevents the beauty of the light from shining through. Make sure that the bulbs have had a chance to cool down, then wipe them with a soft, dry cloth. Don't apply much pressure to the bulb—it may break.

Of course not all overhead lights are chandeliers. You may have traditional fixtures with a flat base attached to the ceiling. You may have track lighting or lights connected to a fan. The glass may be clear, frosted or colored. No matter, it still needs to be cleaned. Remove fixtures carefully. If the light is hard to reach, make sure you use a step stool or ladder to remove it—easier on you, and easier on the light. Keep one hand firmly on or under the fixture while you undo the screws or brackets that hold the fixture to the ceiling, and remove with great care. You don't want to chip the edges.

Now, place an old towel in the bottom of your sink. That should prevent the fixture from hitting the hard bottom and breaking or cracking. Fill the sink with warm water and a little bit of dishwashing liquid. Wash the fixture gently, then remove it from the water and sit it safely to one side on another towel. Empty the sink, then fill it up again with warm water, this time adding ¼ cup of white vinegar. You'll need to put another towel in the water, too. Place the fixture in the sink one last time and leave it there for a minute or so before removing. Gently remove excess moisture with a soft, lint-free cloth, then allow to air-dry thoroughly. Use this dry-time to gently wipe down any metal components with a damp cloth. Buff well with a dry one, and wipe down the lightbulb(s) with a soft cloth. Be sure the fixture is shut off and the bulb and metal are cool. Now you can put the fixture back in place and let the light shine through!

Trick or Treat

Okay, the chores are done and now it's time for fun. And because it's October, that can mean only one thing—Halloween!

THE TREAT

• Makeup is much safer for children than masks, which can obscure their vision.

• Remove glitter makeup and heavy dark makeup from kids' faces with petroleum jelly. Gently work in the jelly (use care with glitter makeup not to get it into the eye area), then tissue away the makeup. Wash face well when done.

• Make sure to leave plenty of room for your child's clothes under the costume. And make sure the costume isn't trailing on the ground. You don't want your child to trip!

• Make sure to check your children's candy before you let them eat it. If little ones are impatient, give them a piece of the candy you bought until you've had time to check the bounty.

• Put some reflective tape on costumes and shoes so that your child will be visible. Consider making a cute flashlight part of the costume.

• Did you color your hair green for Halloween only to discover that the color won't come out? Don't give up hope. Reach for the baking soda, liquid dish soap and shampoo. Make a paste the consistency of thick shampoo, work it well into your hair—concentrate on your hair, not your scalp—then rinse thoroughly. No more green!

THE TRICK

Sometimes those little pirates and princesses come home with a lot more than candy. Here's how to treat those muddy problems.

- When mud gets tracked onto your carpet, don't try to clean it up right away. Cover the wet mud with baking soda; that will absorb the moisture from the mud. Once the mess is dry, vacuum, using only the hose. A beater bar will grind the mud into the carpet, but a hose will concentrate the suction on the muddy area. Finish off with your favorite carpet cleaner.

- Wet mud on your clothes can be treated by flushing the wrong side of the fabric with lots of cool water. Hold the garment under a faucet and direct a forceful stream of water at the clean side of the garment. (Flushing the dirty side with water will only grind the mud into the fabric.) Once the water runs clear, work some Fels-Naptha Heavy Duty Laundry Bar Soap® into the area and launder as usual.

- Muddy shoes should be allowed to dry, then vigorously brushed with a shoe brush. Use fast, downward strokes rather than circular motions, which could grind the mud into the shoes. If mud remains on leather shoes, clean with a bar of soap (Dove® Moisturizing Bath Bar works well) and a soft cloth. Canvas or athletic shoes should be cleaned using Fels-Naptha Soap® and a nailbrush.

- Mud on car upholstery, whether fabric or leather, should be allowed to dry before treating. Use the attachment hose on your vacuum to remove all the mud you can. For fabric upholstery, use your favorite carpet and upholstery cleaner (I like Spot Shot Instant Carpet Stain Remover®), following the directions on the container. On leather, wash the area using a moisturizing bar soap, such as Dove® and wipe with a clean soft cloth.

The Pumpkin Patch

Pumpkins decay and mold quickly, so make sure to put something under your pumpkin, such as a couple of paper plates or a plastic tablecloth. You don't want to have a black stain as a reminder of the holiday.

If you already have a black stain you may be able to remove it with one of the following remedies.

For pumpkin mold on a porch or concrete, try cleaning the area with oven cleaner. Spray the area with the cleaner and allow to sit 10 minutes, then agitate with a brush and rinse well. Do this on a cool day, and make sure to keep kids and pets away.

For wooden tabletops, use a little nongel toothpaste on a damp cloth and rub in a circular motion. You can also try some 0000 steel wool dipped into turpentine. Do this in a very small inconspicuous spot first. Apply some lemon oil to the area when you are done, let it soak in and buff with a soft cloth. You can avoid that stain altogether by making pumpkin pie out of that pumpkin.

Let's Dish!

Dad's Favorite Pumpkin Pie

2 cups canned pumpkin

1 can evaporated milk and ⅓ cup regular milk to equal 2 cups

1 cup granulated sugar

2 eggs, well beaten

½ teaspoon ginger

1 teaspoon cinnamon

½ to ¾ teaspoon nutmeg

½ teaspoon salt

1 deep 8- or 9-inch pie shell

Using a mixer, combine all ingredients thoroughly.

Pour into pie shell. Bake for 15 minutes at 425 degrees, then turn down temperature to 350 degrees and bake until a knife pushed into the center of the pie filling comes out clean, approximately 30 minutes. Serve with whipped cream or nondairy topping.

November

It's November, and the year is almost over! Where did it go? Thank heavens for Thanksgiving and the time to pause, to give thanks for what we have. Thanksgiving is a time of tradition—a big turkey dinner with all the trimmings, Grandmother's silverware, Aunt Jean's china, and Uncle Jim's bad jokes. Nobody wants to keep Jim's bad jokes, but the silverware and china, well that's something we hope to have for a good long time. That's why proper cleaning and maintenance is a must. Take the time to care for these precious heirlooms, and not only will you enjoy them for years to come, but you'll be able to pass them along to your children, your grandchildren, and perhaps even your great-grandchildren! Oh, and when you're finished with the china and silverware, take a moment to get ready for the snow. November is the gateway to winter after all.

Traditions at the Table

THE CHINA SYNDROME

First things first. You'll need to evaluate what you have, so remove everything from the cabinet and place it on the dining table. Don't put the china on a bare table (you could scratch the finish), and don't put it on the floor where you might break something—those *I Love Lucy* situations are best avoided!

Now's the time to get tough. If you're *really* going to repair that teacup—you know, the one that's been broken since the Carter administration—now's the time to do it. If it can't be repaired, and if it doesn't really have any sentimental value, throw it out. Bear in mind that cracked dishes can be unsafe to eat off of because food and debris can settle in the cracks and not come out during washing. If in doubt, throw it out.

If you have a piece of china that has great sentimental value but is broken beyond repair, consider putting it in a sturdy paper bag and giving it a good whack. Collect the pieces (there won't be a million—trust me) and glue them around a picture frame or on a trinket box. Add some jewels, pearls, or artificial flowers, letting your imagination run wild. You'll end up with a lovely keepsake.

Never use the dishwasher for antique china, china with metal trim or hand-painted china.

Dishes that don't get regular use should be cleaned before use. Soap and water will generally do the trick. Just make sure to rinse well. For special challenges, like black cutlery marks on china plates, use nongel toothpaste on a soft cloth to rub the marks away. If you have fine, hairline cracks in old china, soak it in warm milk for 30 to 60 minutes. The cracks should disappear when you remove the plate from the milk. Wash as usual and dry well. If food has left any stains on the china, make a paste of lemon juice and cream of tartar, and rub gently. Rinse the piece well when you're done.

The next step is to dust the cabinet shelves with a soft cloth. Then wash them with a cloth that has been immersed in a mild, soapy solution (1 teaspoon of liquid dish soap to 1 gallon of warm water) and then wrung out until just damp. Wash well and dry thoroughly with a soft, lint-free cloth. You may prefer to wash the shelves with a solution of brewed tea (1 quart of warm water and 1 tea bag). Allow the solution to cool to room temperature and wash the shelves using a soft cloth. Then dry thoroughly. A damp microfiber cloth can also be used.

Glass doors should be cleaned with a solution of 2 parts warm water to 1 part rubbing alcohol. Apply the solution directly to the cloth, then wipe gently in small circular motions. Make sure to clean the corners of the glass, too. Buff with a dry, lint-free cloth.

Never spray glass cleaner directly onto glass doors, picture frames or mirrors. The solution can seep into the wood and can cause damage to the surrounding areas.

Sliding doors have tracks that need to be cleaned from time to time. The crevice attachment on your vacuum cleaner is perfect for this. After you've vacuumed, wash the track with a damp, soapy toothbrush and dry with a soft cloth.

Keep the track and doors running smoothly by rubbing them with a little lemon oil or spraying with some furniture polish.

Okay. You've cleaned your cabinet and evaluated its contents. Now's the time to put everything back. Take stock of what you have before returning items to the shelves. What are your favorite pieces? What do you want to display, and what would you rather conceal? Bear this in mind as you arrange your cabinet. Put larger pieces at the back of the cabinet, smaller items in front. Create groupings. Keep one set of china together, silver together, and crystal together, and so on. Put the things you seldom use in the back or on the shelf that's most difficult to reach, and keep them clean by covering with plastic wrap. Always empty sugar from the china sugar bowl.

Stack dinner plates, dessert plates, saucers and other flat items together, and insert a napkin or paper towel between each one to avoid scratches. Sit groups of these flat items on each other to make the most of your space. Cups are more delicate and easily broken, though, so don't stack them more than two deep. Be creative with your groupings. Try putting some of your old and new pieces together. You may just see things in a whole new light!

If you plan to wash your china in the automatic dishwasher, take one piece (say, a cup) and wash it over the course of a month to determine if it's dishwasher safe. Just leave the cup in the dishwasher and let it run through the wash with your everyday dishes. Take a look at the piece every few days or so. If it appears that the trim is changing color, the pattern is fading or small cracks are occurring, you'll want to stop the experiment. If the piece remains unharmed, you can follow with the rest of your set. For best results, use the "china" or "short" cycle, as well as the "energy saver" or "no heat" drying cycle. (You'll save energy and money, too!) I wish I could tell you another easy test you could try, but there isn't one. If you are buying a large set of china, you might want to consider buying one extra, inexpensive piece to try this dishwasher experiment.

Crystal that stands up securely in the rack can be washed in the dishwasher. It should not lean, lay sideways or hook over the prongs on the dishwasher rack. Don't allow crystal pieces to bump against each other during washing—they'll chip. Avoid water spots on crystal by adding 1 teaspoon of 20 Mule Team™ Borax to your automatic dishwashing detergent.

Place a towel in the bottom of the sink when handwashing crystal. The towel will cushion the crystal and prevent breakage.

When handwashing crystal, wash only a few pieces at a time and make sure not to overload the sink. Crystal should be cleaned in hot water, but not too hot. As a general rule, if the water is too hot for your hands, it's too hot for the crystal. Sudden changes of temperature can cause crystal to crack, so place it sideways into the water instead of bottom first. For a squeaky clean finish, add 1 tablespoon of white vinegar to the water, along with your liquid dish soap.

Crystal should be stored upright, as you would drink from it. A lot of people like to store glasses upside down to prevent dust from accumulating in the goblet or flute, but it's not a good idea. Moisture can be trapped inside the glass, causing damage to the crystal and the shelf on which it's stored.

Cranberry stains on that tablecloth? Remove them with a little Wine Away Red Stain Remover™. Works like a charm.

HI HO SILVER

Acidic foods and their residue can tarnish silver and may even cause it to pit. Salt, egg yolk, fish, broccoli, mayonnaise and mustard are the biggest offenders. Get into the habit of rinsing your silver right after you clear the table. You may not be able to wash the dishes right away—I know it's not *my* idea of an after-dinner treat—but a thorough rinsing will go a long way to prevent permanent damage.

Wash silverware in hot water and mild dishwashing liquid. Rinse well, and dry with a soft, lint-free cloth. Don't allow silver to air-dry, as this can result in water spotting. Silver *must* be dry before storing, so make sure to dry well.

Did you know?

Rubber causes silver to tarnish, so don't dry pieces on a rubber mat or store it wrapped in rubber bands.

• Silverware washed in a dishwasher should never be mixed with stainless steel cutlery. Pitting may occur.

• Never store silver in plastic bags or plastic wrap. That traps condensation and can encourage tarnish.

• Store silver in a tarnish-proof bag or wrap it in acid-free tissue paper. If you wear clean, soft gloves when doing this task, you won't leave finger marks—that's where tarnish can begin.

• For quick silver cleaning, put strips of aluminum foil in a large bowl, place the silver on top of the foil, pour boiling water over the silver and add 3 tablespoons of baking soda. Soak for a few minutes, then rinse and dry. Don't use this method on hollow or glued pieces.

• Rubbing silver with a damp cloth dipped in baking soda will also remove tarnish. Or try a little nongel toothpaste on a soft, damp cloth. Rinse and dry thoroughly before using.

Just boiled some potatoes? Let the water cool and then pour over silver. Allow it to soak for 30 minutes. Wash, rinse and rub with a soft cloth. The starch in the potato water will clean the silver.

• Never store salt in silver saltshakers. This could lead to tarnish.

• Remove tarnish and other stains from the inside of silver coffeepots by rubbing with a fine piece of steel wool dipped in white vinegar and salt. Use grade 0000.

• Place several sugar cubes in a silver coffeepot before storing, and you'll never have an old, musty smell. The Queen Mum taught me that one!

• Store silver teapots and coffeepots with the lid open or off so that moisture is never trapped inside.

• Clean the inside of silver teapots by filling with water to which you have added a small handful of Arm and Hammer Washing Soda™. Let soak overnight, rinse and dry well.

• Clean silver-plated items as you would real silver, but be gentle—silver plating can rub off.

• Cleaning silver is important, but be careful not to rub too hard on the hallmark. If you wear it off or distort it, the value of the set will be reduced.

Silver takes on a beautiful patina with age and with use—rather like a Queen!—so don't just keep it stored away in a drawer. A beautifully set table is an important part of a holiday meal, and your silverware is a meaningful part of that setting. So use your silverware, treat it well, and each time you set the table you'll have beautiful memories to enjoy.

If someone spills gravy on your tablecloth during dinner, sprinkle the spill with baking soda or salt to absorb it and enjoy the rest of the meal. After dinner, treat with Zout® Stain Remover and launder as usual.

There's No Business Like Snow Business

So you're thinking *What does a woman in Arizona know about snow?* Well, I lived in Michigan for more than forty years (we don't have to go into details here), so believe me, I know what I'm talking about when I talk snow!

GIVE SNOW AND SALT THE BOOT

• Keep boots looking their best by applying a good coat of quality paste polish and following up with a spray of water protectant.

• Damp or wet boots should be dried standing up. A roll of cardboard or a bent wire hanger will help them keep their shape. Never allow boots to dry on a heat register—the leather could crack.

• Remove salt stains by wiping with a mixture of 1 part water and 1 part white vinegar.

Buttons on heavy winter coats have to do double duty, what with that heavy fabric and the constant on-and-off as you go from indoors to out. Try sewing them on with dental floss instead. It's stronger and longer-lasting than most thread, so you'll never be bothered with missing buttons again. If your coat is dark, just finish off with a few loops of dark thread to avoid an ugly contrast.

CAR DETAIL

• Don't wait until it's too late. Schedule a tune-up and winterizing appointment for your car.

• Give your car a thorough cleaning before the winter sets in. Don't forget to vacuum the carpet and upholstery, and treat it with a good-quality fabric protector.

• Make sure the dashboard and defroster are clear from obstructions.

• Rubber mats with deep, diagonal grooves really help to capture melting snow. They're a good investment.

• Locks frozen in your car? If your car is in the garage near an electrical outlet, use a blow-dryer on the low setting to direct the warm air into the lock, from a distance of about six inches. That should do the trick. If your car is outside, heat your key with a match or lighter and insert it into the lock. Leave it there for a few minutes, and then gently turn the key. You may have to do this a few times, but it should work. *Don't try this method if your lock has an electronic device.* You could damage the chip.

• Rub Vaseline™ on the gaskets so doors don't freeze.

Prevent frozen locks in your car by covering the lock with a couple layers of masking tape. The tape will keep the lock free from moisture, and that's what causes the ice to form.

• Getting stuck in the snow can be a real pain in the radials, so keep a bag of Kitty Litter™ in your trunk for some much-needed traction. A few layers of newspaper work well, too.

• Don't run out of windshield washer fluid. One part rubbing alcohol to 1 part water, and a few drops of liquid dish soap, work well on winter windshields. And if you treat them first with Clean Shield® protectant, they'll be that much easier to clean. Snow and grime will wipe right off.

• You can shave a few minutes off your morning snow detail if you place an old beach towel on the windshield the night before a forecasted snowfall. Tuck the towel beneath the windshield wipers before the snowfall, pull it off afterward, and you won't have to scrape your windows. Just give the towel a good shake and dream of sunnier days. A mitten placed on your sideview mirror will save you time, too!

• It's always a good idea to keep an emergency kit in your car during winter. Nobody leaves the house saying, "I think I'll get stuck in the snow today," so be prepared. Take along the following:

> Blanket
> Flashlight and some extra batteries
> Two bottles of water
> Chocolate bar (for emergencies only!)
> Piece of red cloth to tie to the car

SHOVEL IT

Every year hundreds of people suffer heart attacks from shoveling snow. Follow these simple rules to minimize the hazards.

- Never shovel snow after a heavy meal.
- Dress in layers and always wear a hat.
- Don't shovel snow after you've been drinking.
- Don't overload your shovel—snow can be very heavy.
- Always bend from the knees.
- Make sure someone knows where you are.
- Pace yourself. Take frequent breaks.

Give your snow shovel a coat of nonstick cooking spray before you start to tackle the driveway. You won't be bothered with those annoying clumps that stick to the shovel!

❄️ December 🎄

Christmas comes but once a year, which is a good thing if you're the one who has to do all the work. Try to make Christmas as stress-free as possible by planning ahead and enlisting what help you can. Don't be a holiday hero. Involve even the youngest members of your family, and don't decline those offers of help. Make lists. Plan ahead and try not to abandon your family's routine. The closer you follow yours—regular mealtimes and bedtimes, for example—the more you'll be able to enjoy the excitement of Christmas without the chaos. So go ahead and deck those halls . . . just don't forget to dust them first.

Holiday Hints

TEN TIME SAVERS

1. Tell your children that Santa only comes to a clean house. Don't laugh—it worked on me for years!

2. Take the time to clean your house *before* you bring in the tree and all the decorations. Sure, you'll probably need a quick vacuum once you have the tree in place, but it's easier to clean a house when you don't have to

maneuver all those holiday adornments around. Trust me on this one.

3. Make lists and stick to them. It's amazing how much time and effort you'll save.

4. Never say no to those offers of "Can I bring something?" or "Can I help?"

5. Shop early in the morning or late at night when stores aren't as crowded. Make use of the Internet and catalogs whenever possible.

6. Consider these quick gifts: a phone card, a wine club membership, a framed photo of a special time, this book, a gift certificate for a favorite coffeehouse, and pretty stationery with stamps.

7. Use gift bags instead of wrapping paper.

8. Make your own frozen dinners by preparing extra portions when you're cooking a big meal. Great for dinner when you're rushed, and great for the kids when you're on your way out to a party.

9. Get your holiday clothes cleaned and ready in advance. Hang the clothes and accessories together and you will have time for a leisurely bath, too!

10. Remove the word "perfection" from your vocabulary.

IT'S A FAMILY AFFAIR

• Enlist the whole family in a quick cleanup. Small children can dust, older ones can vacuum, your spouse can do the dishes, and you can tidy up and put things away. It's amazing what you can accomplish in thirty short minutes.

• Involve children in sending out Christmas cards. Older

ones can address the envelopes, and little ones can lick the stamps!

• Let your children bake some Christmas cookies. They're easy to prepare and require little supervision—just make sure to keep small hands away from the oven. You can make things easier by giving cookie cutters a quick spritz of non-stick cooking spray to prevent dough from clinging. And for those stubborn cookies that won't come away from the baking sheet? Slide a length of dental floss under each cookie and they'll glide right off.

• Children love to make pictures with artificial snow, but it can be difficult to wash off. Prevent snow from sticking by preparing the surface with a light misting of nonstick cooking spray. If you forget this step you can still remove it easily: Just rub with a little bit of white, nongel toothpaste.

• Let the kids wrap some gifts. The outcome may not be just as you'd like, but the kids will have fun and they'll be proud of their accomplishment.

O' CHRISTMAS TREE

• Know the height of your living room before you select your tree. Make sure to allow for the stand (about a foot) and the treetop. Size does matter!

• Older trees are dry and will drop needles when shaken, so make sure to shake the tree before you buy it. Choose one that has sturdy, flexible needles and a strong, fresh scent.

• The first thing to do when you bring your tree home is to cut off a small diagonal section at the base of the trunk. Trees need a lot of water, and this small act will help them to absorb it.

• Pine tree needles will last longer if spritzed first with fabric sizing or spray starch. Just make sure to do this *before* you put the lights on.

• Put a plastic tablecloth under the base of your tree to help protect your carpet from spills.

• If you do have a spill from your Christmas tree, clean it up as soon as possible or you'll have mold on the carpet. Slide the tree carefully to one side, and blot up all of the water by standing on some heavy towels placed on the carpet. Absorb all you can. Clean the area with your favorite carpet cleaner, and let a fan blow across the area until it is thoroughly dry, at least 24 hours.

Nourish your Christmas tree with a mixture of 1 quart of water, 2 tablespoons of lemon juice, 1 tablespoon of sugar and ½ teaspoon of liquid bleach. If you want a simpler solution, try 2 ounces of Listerine® or 1 tablespoon of maple syrup.

• Add water to the reservoir of a Christmas tree with a turkey baster, and you'll keep spills to a minimum.

• Make sure to water your tree daily.

• Rub a little petroleum jelly on the trunk of your artificial tree before inserting the branches. They'll be easier to remove in the new year.

• Put lights on your tree before adding any other decorations. And when choosing your lights, remember that white bulbs give off more light than colored ones.

• Ran out of hooks and hangers? Use paper clips, bobby pins, twist ties, pipe cleaners or dental floss. These makeshift hooks work well, but they're not very attractive, so try putting these ornaments deeper in the tree, where you're less likely to see the fastener.

Protect your door by securing a piece of weather stripping under your wreath.

AT THE TABLE

• Finding your good napkins wrinkled from storage can be frustrating. Don't despair. Just throw them in the dryer, along with a damp towel. After 10 minutes or so the creases will relax and you won't have to iron them.

• Don't throw away those empty rolls of wrapping paper. If you make a slit down the side of the roll and slide it over a coat hanger, you can use it to hang tablecloths without worrying about creases.

Put a few layers of foil in the basket before you add the napkin and rolls. Your bread and buns will stay warmer longer. Just about everybody likes warm buns!

• Clean your dining table the natural way, with tea! Make a pot of tea. Sit down, have a cup yourself, and wait until the tea is cool to the touch. Pour the liquid into a small container, saturate a clean, lint-free cloth, and wring it out till barely damp. Then wipe the table and leaves in the direction of the wood grain. Buff dry with a soft, dry cloth.

The Cat's Meow

Christmas may be an exciting time for people, but it can be a little nerve-racking for those of us with four legs. Here are a few things to watch out for:

- Holiday plants such as holly, poinsettia and mistletoe can be toxic. Please keep them away from us—and from small children, too.

- Cats love to play with tinsel, but we also like to eat it. This can wreak havoc on our intestinal tract. Please keep the tinsel and other stringy decorations out of our reach. If you want to put tinsel on the tree, avoid the lower branches.

- We may like to eat rich foods, but they're not good for us and can make us sick, especially chocolate. If you can't resist our soulful faces staring up at you while you're eating dinner, give us some carrots and a small piece of turkey without gravy. Of course, it's best not to feed us from the table at all, but don't ever say I told you that!

- Bear in mind that I may not be the party animal you think I am. If you're having lots of company, please put me in a room by myself, with my food, water and litter box. Better include a chew toy for the dog—you know how they get . . .

Zack

• Remove white marks from your table with a little bit of mayonnaise. Just make sure it's regular mayonnaise— low-fat won't do the trick. Mix the mayonnaise with table salt or cigarette ash. Massage the mixture into the mark for about 45 minutes. Yes, 45 minutes! It's a long time, but it's the massaging that gently buffs the mark away. Allow the mixture to sit for several hours, preferably overnight. Linseed oil and rottenstone (both available in hardware stores) work well, too.

• Use wax sticks or crayons to cover scratches. Make sure you get these from the hardware or furniture store (your child's crayons won't work here), and take care to match the shade of the stick to the table. Once you've applied the crayon according to the manufacturer's instructions, heat the area with a blow-dryer and buff firmly with an old rag for an almost invisible repair.

IT'S A WRAP

• Keep rolls of wrapping paper handy by standing them up in a wastebasket or in a small, clean garbage can.

• Empty wrapping paper rolls can also be used as kindling. Slide small twigs, dried leaves and broken bits of pinecones in the tubes to make the foundation of a wonderful, crackling fire.

Be creative when wrapping packages. Fabric, wallpaper, maps, tee shirts and sheet music all make great gift coverings.

• Run out of wrapping paper? Recycle some old gift wrap by spraying the back with spray starch. Press with a warm iron and you're ready to go!

• Keep the end of the tape from disappearing by folding it over a paper clip. You'll never have to pick at bits of tape again.

• Don't burn foil wrapping or magazines in a fireplace— they emit noxious, dangerous gases.

• Recycled Christmas cards make great gift tags.

That Oh-So Common Cold

Christmas may be a time of giving, but nobody wants a cold. Here are some things to minimize your chances of getting this seasonal nuisance. If you do get a cold, look here for some comforting remedies . . . and some solutions for the stains those remedies can cause on your soft flannel sheets!

AN OUNCE OF PREVENTION

• Contrary to the old wives' tale, you can't catch cold from being out in the cold weather. Colds are caused by viruses. Avoid the virus, avoid the cold.

Help prevent colds by washing your hands for as long as it takes to sing "Happy Birthday" . . . twice! That's the amount of time you'll need to wash your hands properly.

• Wash your hands frequently and wash them well. Use water that is comfortably hot. *Always* use soap.

• Avoid touching your eyes, nose and mouth.

• Use tissues instead of handkerchiefs, if at all possible. Tissues are more easily disposed of, along with their germs!

• Don't leave tissues in an open trash can. Dispose of them in a plastic bag kept just for that purpose. You don't want anyone else picking up your germs!

• Try not to share things with someone who is ill. That includes towels, glasses and cooking utensils.

Be particularly vigilant about sharing phones. Use a soft cloth dipped in Listerine® Mouthwash or rubbing alcohol to swab down phone mouthpieces, door handles and computer keyboards. Alcohol wipes work well, too.

• Continue to share kisses—there's nothing like a little love when you're sick. Just confine it to the cheeks.

COLD CARE

• Keep your feet warm. Believe it or not, cold feet can cause your nostrils to become cold and dry, and that can aggravate your cold.

• Wash bedding and pajamas in the hottest possible water.

• The fragrance of fabric softener can irritate delicate noses, so soften flannel sheets and cotton towels with ¼ cup of white vinegar when you have a cold.

Make sure you check the date on those cold medicines before you take them.

• Rubbing some Vicks Vapor Rub® on the outside of your throat and chest will soothe that congestion, no matter how old you are.

• Put a dash of wintergreen oil in a basin of hot water, lower your face to the water (no closer than twelve inches, though), and put a towel over your head to create a tent. Breathe deeply for some much-needed relief.

Prone to cold sores? Dab on some Pepto Bismol® when you feel that first tingle, and chances are the sore won't make an appearance!

HUMIDIFIER HEAVEN

Moist air is heaven to dry throats and nasal passages, but if you don't keep your humidifier clean and free from mold, you may find your cold aggravated by airborne pollutants.

Remove mineral deposits from detachable parts, such as the plastic rotor tube and locking ring, by submerging them in a pot of hot white vinegar. Bring a pot of vinegar to boil, remove it from the stove, and then immerse the tube and ring in the vinegar for about five minutes. Rinse well in clear water and make sure that all parts are dry before returning them to the unit.

Clean a humidifier by swishing around a solution of 1 cup of bleach in 1 gallon of water in the container that holds the water, allowing it to soak for a few minutes, if necessary. Scrub any mineral deposits with a brush and then rinse. Make sure the humidifier is cool and empty before you start.

WHAT TO DO FOR THOSE COLD MEDICATION STAINS

Rubs, liniments, eardrops and ointments are oil-based stains, so you should treat these as soon as you can. Rubbing the stain with a good waterless hand cleaner such as GOJO Crème Waterless Hand Cleaner™ is your best bet. Apply directly to the stain, and rub it in well with your thumb and forefinger. Wait 10 minutes, then apply a good stain remover, such as Zout®, before laundering in the hottest possible water.

Baby wipes are great for removing stains caused by medicated ointments. Rub the stained fabric firmly with the baby wipe, then pretreat and launder as usual.

Cough syrups and other red-based stains can be removed quite effectively with Wine Away Red Wine Stain Remover™ or Red Erase™. Apply liberally, as directed on the container, then launder as usual. Alternatively, soak the stained area in 1 cup of warm water and 1 tablespoon of salt.

Fabric stained from hot toddies and medicated drinks should be flushed under cool, running water as soon as possible. Be sure to direct the water to the *wrong* side of the fabric. Next, make a paste with 20 Mule Team® Borax and cool water. Use about 2 parts borax to 1 part water, adding more water as needed to create a pastelike consistency. Apply to the fabric, then have a cup of tea and watch your favorite sitcom. Once 30 minutes have passed, it's time to loosen the mixture by applying more cool water. Work the loosened mixture between your thumb and forefinger, then launder as usual in the hottest possible water for the fabric type.

Americans suffer from more than one billion colds a year. That's nothing to sneeze at!

Let's Dish!

Mom made these cookies every year for as long as I can remember. When I got old enough I got to "help"—I loved the decorating part best and I admit to sneaking a bite of the dough, not a healthy thing to do.

The Queen Mother's Christmas Cookies

2 cups flour
1 teaspoon baking powder
½ teaspoon baking soda
½ teaspoon salt
½ cup shortening
1 cup sugar
¼ teaspoon nutmeg
¼ teaspoon lemon extract or grated rind
2 eggs

Mix together the dry ingredients in a bowl.

Using a mixer, cream together the shortening, sugar, nutmeg and lemon extract until well blended and light in color. Beat in the eggs and add the dry ingredients a little at a time, beating between additions.

Chill the mixture in the refrigerator for an hour or so, and then bake in one of the following ways:

Roll out the dough and cut with cookie cutters and place on a greased cookie sheet.

Drop by rounded tablespoons onto a greased cookie sheet and flatten with the bottom of a drinking glass dipped in flour.

Decorate the cookies by placing a raisin or nut in the center. Sprinkle with granulated sugar—colored granulated sugar is nice for Christmas.

Bake in a 375-degree oven for 10 to 12 minutes. Do not overbake. Makes about 3 dozen cookies.

Think I'll go call my mom . . .

Resource Guide

ACT NATURAL™ CLOTHS: See Euronet USA.

AT HOME ALL-PURPOSE CLEANER®: See Soapworks®.

BORAX: Better known as 20 Mule Team® Borax, this laundry additive can be found in the detergent aisle.

BRILLIANT BLEACH®: See Soapworks®.

CALGON WATER SOFTENER®: Look for it with the laundry additives at the grocery store.

CHAMOIS: Found in hardware stores and home centers.

CHARCOAL: This is the type made for fish tanks and is available at pet supply stores.

CLEAN SHIELD® SURFACE TREATMENT (formerly Invisible Shield®): This is such a wonderful product—just the name gives me goose bumps! It turns all of those hard-to-clean surfaces in your home (tub, shower, shower doors, sinks, counters, stovetops, windows, any surface that is not wood or painted) into nonstick surfaces that can be cleaned with water and a soft cloth. No more soap scum or hard-water deposits! It never builds up on surfaces so it won't make them slippery, and it's nontoxic, so you can use it on dishes and food surfaces, too. Call 1-800-528-3149 to find a supplier near you.

CLEAR AMMONIA: There are two types of ammonia, clear and sudsy (sometimes called "cloudy"). Clear contains no soap and should be used where suggested for that reason.

CUTICLE REMOVER: The gel you apply to your cuticles to soften them. Let's be clear, it is cuticle remover, NOT nail polish remover.

DENATURED ALCOHOL: This is an industrial alcohol reserved for heavy-duty cleaning. Don't use it near an open flame, and dispose of any rags that were used to apply it outside the home. Launder or clean anything that you treat with it as soon as possible. Look for this in cans at hardware stores and home centers. Remember the Queen's rule: always test in an inconspicuous place before treating a large area with this product.

ENERGINE CLEANING FLUID®: A great spotter. Look for this at the hardware store, the home center and even in some grocery stores (usually on the top shelf with the laundry additives).

EPSOM SALTS: Usually used for medicinal purposes, but handy for household uses, too. Look for it in drugstores.

EURONET USA: Makers of the ACT Natural™ Microfiber Cloths and Mops. They clean and disinfect without chemicals, using only water. They have been scientifically proven to kill germs and bacteria and even come with a warranty. They are easy to use, great for people with allergies, and can be cleaned and sanitized in the washer (this is particularly important with the mop). Use them in the kitchen, bathroom, to spot carpet, on windows, mirrors, hard furniture, in the car, virtually anywhere you clean. Call 1-888-638-2882 or visit www.euronetusa.com. They are a wonderful investment. My mop is almost two years old and is still doing the job.

FELS-NAPTHA SOAP®: What a wonderful laundry spotter and

cleaner this is. You'll find it in the bar soap section of the grocery store. It's usually on the bottom shelf in a small stack and always has dust on it, because nobody knows what to use it for. Call 1-800-45PUREX.

FINE STEEL WOOL: Look for the symbol "0000" and the word "fine." And don't try soap-filled steel wool pads. They are not acceptable substitutes.

FRESH BREEZE LAUNDRY SOAP®: See Soapworks®.

GLYCERIN: Look for glycerin in drugstores in the hand cream section. Always purchase plain glycerin, not the type containing rose water.

GOJO CRÈME WATERLESS HAND CLEANER™: People with greasy hands have used this product for years. It's a hand cleaner and so much more. Look for it at home centers and hardware stores.

HYDROGEN PEROXIDE: Choose the type that you use on cuts and to gargle with—not the type used to bleach hair. That will remove color from carpet or fabric.

LINSEED OIL: You'll find this at the hardware store, usually in the paint and staining section. It is combustible, so use care in disposing of rags or paper towels used to apply it. Keep it in the garage or basement away from open flame.

MEAT TENDERIZER: Use the unseasoned variety please, or you will have a whole new stain to deal with. Store brands work fine.

NAIL POLISH REMOVER: I caution you to use nonacetone polish remover, which is much less aggressive than acetone polish remover. (Straight acetone is exceedingly strong.) Use only where recommended and with great care. Look for this product at beauty supply stores.

NATURAL SPONGE: A natural sponge is the best sponge you will ever use. It has hundreds of natural "scrubbing fingers" that make any wall-washing job speed by. Look for these at home centers and hardware stores and choose a nice size to fit your hand. Wash them in lukewarm water with gentle suds. You can put them in the washing machine if you avoid combining them with fabrics that have lint.

NONGEL TOOTHPASTE: This is just a fancy name for old-fashioned plain white toothpaste. Gels just don't work, so don't even try.

ODORZOUT™: A fabulous, dry, 100 percent natural deodorizer. It's nontoxic, so you can use it anyplace you have a smell or a stink. It is especially effective on pet urine odors, and since it is used dry it is simple to apply. Call 1-800-88STINK, or visit their website at www.88stink.com.

PREPARATION H®: Sold in drugstores. An ointment intended for hemorrhoids.

PUREX® LAUNDRY DETERGENT: Available wherever detergents are sold or call 1-800-45PUREX for a location near you.

RED ERASE®: Made by the same people who make Wine Away Red Wine Stain Remover™, Red Erase™ is for red stains such as red pop, grape juice, grape jelly, etc. Look for it at Linens 'n Things, or call 1-888-WINEAWAY for a store location near you.

RUST REMOVER: These are serious products, so follow the directions carefully. Look for products like Whink® and Rust Magic® at hardware stores and home centers.

SHAVING CREAM: The cheaper brands work fine, and shaving cream works better than gel.

SOAPWORKS®: Manufacturer of wonderful nontoxic, user- and earth-friendly cleaning, laundry, and personal care products. Try their At Home All-Purpose Cleaner®, originally designed for allergy and asthma sufferers. Soapworks® products are very effective, and they are economical, so everyone can use them. Call 1-800-699-9917 or visit their website at www.soapworks.com.

SOOT AND DIRT REMOVAL SPONGE: These are used to clean walls, wallpaper, lampshades and even soot. They also remove pet hair from upholstery. These big brick erasers are available at home centers and hardware stores, usually near the wallpaper supplies. Clean them by washing in a pail of warm water and liquid dish soap, rinse well and allow to dry before using again.

SPOT SHOT INSTANT CARPET STAIN REMOVER®: My all-time favorite carpet spotter and I have tried them all! Try SPOT SHOT UPHOLSTERY STAIN REMOVER® too. Available most everywhere, or call 1-800-848-4389.

SQUEEGEE: When buying a squeegee for washing windows, look for a good quality one with a replaceable rubber blade. Always be sure that the rubber blade is soft and flexible for best results. Look for these at hardware stores, home centers and janitorial supply companies. They come in different widths, so be sure to think about the size windows, etc., that you are going to use it for. A 12-inch blade is a good starting point.

TANG™ BREAKFAST DRINK: Yes, this is the product that the astronauts took to the moon! It is also a great cleaner. (Store brands work just as well.)

TRISODIUM PHOSPHATE (TSP): Cleaning professionals have used this product for years. It is wonderful for washing walls, garage floors and any tough cleaning job. Look for it at hardware stores, home centers and janitorial supply stores. Wear rubber gloves when using it.

TYPEWRITER ERASER: A thing of the past, but still available at office supply stores. Shaped like a pencil with a little brush where the pencil eraser would be, they can be sharpened like a pencil and will last for years.

UN-DU™: Removes sticky residue from fabric and hard surfaces. Look for it at office supply stores, home center stores and hardware stores.

WASHING SODA: I like Arm and Hammer® Washing Soda, which can be found in the detergent aisle at the grocery store along with other laundry additives. No, you cannot substitute baking soda, it is a different product!

WAX CRAYONS: These are sold in hardware stores and home centers and come in various wood colors for concealing scratches in wood surfaces. Don't be fooled by the color name; try to take along a sample of what you need to patch to get the best possible match.

WD-40® LUBRICANT: I bet you will find a can in your garage or basement. Fine spray oil for lubricating all kinds of things, it's a wonderful product for regenerating grease so that it can be removed from clothes. Look for WD-40® at the hardware store, home center and even the grocery store.

WINE AWAY RED WINE STAIN REMOVER™: This unbelievable product can remove red stains, such as red wine, red pop, cranberry juice, red food coloring, grape juice, etc., from carpet and fabric. It is totally nontoxic and made from fruit and vegetable extracts. I just can't believe how well it works! Look for it where liquor is sold or call 1-888-WINEAWAY for a store location near you.

WITCH HAZEL: An astringent/toning product sold at drugstores.

ZOUT® STAIN REMOVER: A very versatile laundry prespotter, Zout® is thicker than most laundry spotters, so you can target the spot. It really works! Look for it in grocery stores and places like Kmart, etc.

NOW YOU CAN TALK DIRTY WITH
The Queen of Clean®
EVERY OTHER MONTH!

If you enjoyed the book, you're sure to enjoy a subscription to QUEEN OF CLEAN®—The Newsletter for just $19.50 per year. You'll receive 6 issues, one every other month. Each 8-page issue is loaded with cleaning information, tips and answers to subscriber questions. Just send your order to the address below and the Queen will start your subscription immediately!

Now Available—Other Queen of Clean Products!

Plus, you can order these products tested and approved by the Queen herself. Each one designed to make cleaning chores a little less, well, dirty.

TELESCOPING LAMBSWOOL DUSTER (Item #101)

Washable dusters will last up to 10 years depending on care and usage. Use on fans, lights, furniture, blinds, ceilings, baseboards, everything! Only $12 each plus $3.95 shipping and handling.

LAMBSWOOL DUST MITT (Item #102)

Never use dusting chemicals again with this over-the-hand duster. See the beauty that the lanolin in the duster can bring to your hard surfaces. Lasts up to 10 years and easily washes clean. A must to simplify all your dusting chores. Only $10 each plus $3 shipping and handling.

PALACE POTTY PUFF (Item #103)

The answer to your toilet cleaning problems! It lasts for years and won't scratch or rust. Can be disinfected with a little chlorine bleach in your toilet bowl. Self-wringing so your hands never touch the water. Only $4.50 each plus $3 shipping and handling.

QUEEN OF CLEAN® APRON (Item #104)

Royal blue twill-type fabric with full pockets across the front, ties at neck and waist for custom fit. Across the front, in yellow letters with red shadowing, it says, "TALK DIRTY TO ME." Beneath that, in smaller letters, it declares, "I Know the Queen of Clean!" Perfect for a woman, or as a barbecue apron for a man. Only $12 each plus $3 shipping and handling.

Check or credit card orders only, please! Be sure to provide your name, address and telephone number so we can contact you in the event of any questions about your order.

If ordering by credit card, please include card type (VISA, MasterCard), account number, expiration date and your signature along with the item number(s) and the required shipping and handling charges plus applicable sales tax to:

QUEEN OF CLEAN
PO BOX 655
PEORIA, AZ 85380

Or order at **www.queenofclean.com**   Thank you for your order!